THE TRAIL OF PAINTED PONIES

ZON INTERNATIONAL PUBLISHING
HORSEPOWER NEW MEXICO
SANTA FE • NEW MEXICO

Eduardo Fuss, photo

HorsePower New Mexico, 102 E Water Street, Suite 5, Santa Fe, NM 87501
Phone: 505-955-9595

www.gopaintedponies.com

Published for HorsePower New Mexico, LLC by
ZON INTERNATIONAL PUBLISHING COMPANY• SANTA FE, NM

Designed by William Manns and Laurel Avery

ISBN 0-939549-45-X

Library of Congress catalog #2001094255

Printed in Hong Kong

TABLE OF CONTENTS

Eduardo Fuss, photo

Shelley Heatley, photo

The Land of Enchantment became a little more wondrous this summer thanks to the exciting public art project, The Trail of Painted Ponies. In every sense, this is genuinely a New Mexico project. The artist who designed the original form for the ponies is a Santa Fe sculptor. An Albuquerque company cast the ponies in polyurethane and the artists who transformed the horses into stunning works of art are from communities across the state.

I support this project because it sets an inspiring example of what can be accomplished through teamwork. A majority of the project was underwritten by the businesses and organizations that "ponied" up the sponsorship money because they felt this project offered them an innovative way to market themselves, while helping their favorite cause. It offered artists a unique opportunity to exhibit their talents, and promote their careers. But perhaps most importantly, it presented social, cultural, educational, animal, philanthropic and charitable organizations around the state with a totally new and different way of raising monies. It represents a terrific win-win situation for all involved.

In addition to bringing diverse facets of the community together, this project offers visitors of our state a memorable experience. With six Painted Ponies corralled at the Albuquerque Sunport, everyone who arrives in New Mexico by air realizes they have landed in a special place, a place that values the arts, and sees the arts as a way of learning about our history and cultural heritage. When they learn that ponies are being exhibited in nine different communities, I hope they will consider taking a "trail drive" around the state.

HorsePower New Mexico deserves a big thank you for their efforts in planning, organizing and realizing this event. The importance of independent projects, undertaken by enterprising young organizations that see an opportunity, take the initiative, and find a way to make it happen, cannot be overestimated.

Sincerely,

Gary E. Johnson
Governor

Eduardo Fuss, photos

El Vado, detail
Chrissie Orr

THE TALE OF THE TRAIL

Imagine a remuda of over 100 horses stretched from Carlsbad to Roswell to Albuquerque to Santa Fe and Taos. Picture them grazing along old Route 66, some in parks and plazas, bank and hotel lobbies, others tethered to hitching posts in front of businesses. Now summon up an image of them painted in day-glo colors, sporting outrageous trappings, so transformed they could have broken free from a carousel, or escaped a madcap circus, and run wild across the New Mexico landscape.

With this vision in mind, Santa Fe author Rodney Barker conceived and organized The Trail of Painted Ponies, a public art extravaganza that has given new meaning to the term Land of Enchantment.

A SLOW START

It was not a vision that was immediately grasped by everyone. After witnessing the phenomenal popularity of CowParade in Chicago—a public art project that brought visitors and revenues in the millions to the city, then raised equal amounts for charity—Barker approached city and state arts councils, encouraging them to undertake a similar project in New Mexico. It seemed like a natural. New Mexico's economy depended on tourism. The state was home to a world-class art community. Many of the state's charities depended on the generosity of fellow citizens, and this represented an innovative way for them to raise new monies.

Moreover, New Mexico had a national reputation as a center of creativity. There was enormous appeal in the idea of mounting a unified art exhibition based on the diverse ideas of a variety of major artists.

Barker's enthusiasm was met with skepticism. No existing arts organizations wanted to become involved.

They had other projects going on. A statewide effort presented enormous logistical challenges. Multi-city projects meant multiple bureaucratic lines had to be crossed.

Continuing to believe the concept had possibilities, Barker formed a core group of artists, patrons and volunteers, and together they fashioned a version of what happened in Chicago that fit the New Mexico economic and cultural landscape.

Three decisions came out of those early meetings:
1) Rather than cows, New Mexico should feature horses. After all, it was through New Mexico that Spanish conquistadores introduced the horse to North America, five centuries ago. Also, the horse was a multi-cultural icon, and New Mexico was a multi-cultural state.
2) Instead of limiting the project to one city it should be a statewide effort, giving artists in communities around New Mexico the opportunity to exhibit their talent.
3) To show people how the project would work, a miniature show should take place first, held in the summer of 2000.

A MINIATURE SHOW

Thirty-three artists were invited to paint, decorate, and aesthetically enhance a small horse, approximately 10"x12", cast in epoxy resin. The design for the horse was generously donated by Star Liana York, a Santa Fe sculptor with a national reputation. The New Mexico Office of Cultural Affairs arranged for an opening at the Governor's Gallery in the State Capitol. Two weeks later the horses were auctioned off at the Museum of Fine Arts. And to everyone's amazement, nearly $50,000 was raised for two non-profits, one that offered therapeutic horse riding programs to handicapped people, another that supported arts programs in the Santa Fe elementary schools.

With that success to build on, the larger project should have come easily. But skepticism persisted, making it apparent that if the project were to become a reality, Barker, his artist friends, and a few like-minded souls who were volunteering their time would have to come up with a way to make it happen on their own.

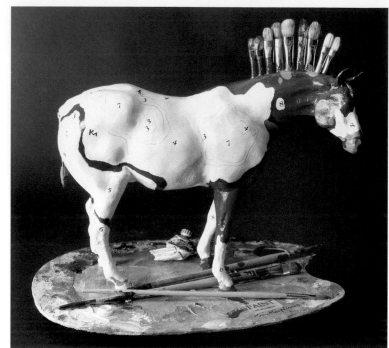

Paint by Numbers, Kevin MacPherson   Eduardo Fuss, photo

Wound-Up Time on the Range, Roger Evans   Eduardo Fuss, photo

Sky of Enchantment, Ilsa Magener   Eduardo Fuss, photo

8

Fireman Pony, A-1 Master Mold & Casting

Eduardo Fuss, photo

The Great Wave, Mary Sweet

Eduardo Fuss, photo

Cloud Prancer, Ron Olguin

Eduardo Fuss, photo

THE PACE PICKS UP

When things are meant to be, help comes from unexpected places. This describes the series of events and parade of people whose combined efforts moved the project from a walk through a trot to a canter.

Barker formed an organization to mount the event. He named his company HorsePower New Mexico and dubbed the project The Trail of Painted Ponies. The way it worked, companies doing business in New Mexico, civic groups and even private individuals were invited to "sponsor" a horse. For $5,000 they received the right to select an artist and design, have a say in the placement of "their" pony, enjoy the promotional benefits that flowed from participation, and they were given the right to select a cultural, social, educational, philanthropic, or animal organization to receive the net proceeds when the ponies went up for sale at the end of the project. The only condition was the beneficiary had to have non-profit status and be New Mexico-based. HorsePower would provide the artist with a "horse canvas"

9

to paint, pay the artist a minimum $1200 honorarium, publicize the project locally and nationally, and conduct the auction.

The concept sounded intriguing enough that the New Mexico Department of Tourism invited Barker to speak at its annual industry retreat. There, he stressed three main points: The Trail of Painted Ponies would diversify tourism, providing the state

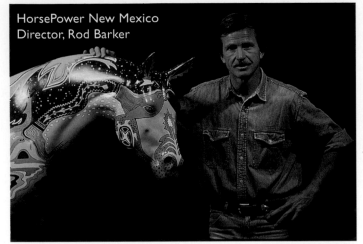

HorsePower New Mexico
Director, Rod Barker

Eduardo Fuss, photo

with a major new attraction. It would give businesses a new way of marketing themselves at the same time that it supported the arts. And, it would fund-raise for a wide range of worthy causes.

After that session, the pace of things picked up. To kick-start the project, Star York offered to enlarge her horse design to life-size and share the costs of the mold. An Albuquerque company, A-1 Master Mold and Casting Services, expressed interest in casting the horses in durable polyurethane. The publisher of Southwest Art magazine volunteered to run a series of ads asking artists to submit designs, which led to hundreds of proposals from around the state and distant parts of the country. Several purchasers of the small horses expressed their interest in sponsoring life-size horses. The New Mexico media got excited, and newspapers and television stations began to cover the project. Recognizing its potential to bolster a sense of community, Mayors Larry Delgado of Santa Fe and Jim Baca of Albuquerque officially endorsed The Trail of Painted Ponies. Other communities, namely Carlsbad and Roswell, joined the effort, seeing it as an opportunity to put themselves on the art map of New Mexico. Congressman Tom Udall showed up at a HorsePower-sponsored opening to congratulate it for taking an initiative that combined art and commerce in a fresh way....

By the end of the year, The Trail of Painted Ponies was gathering momentum.

THE ARTISTIC RESPONSE

From the start, it was important to HorsePower that the artwork exhibited in The Trail of Painted Ponies maintain a high standard of quality and diversity. The organization wanted this event to be distinctive. Achieving that goal began with the form of the horse. HorsePower was approached by several companies that produced fiberglass horses for theme parks and tack stores, but after careful consideration a decision was made that there were advantages to producing its own horse image, created by a New Mexico sculptor uniquely for this project. For a sculptor of Star York's stature to create an original design for artists to paint also gave the project a creatively collaborative character.

The next decision involved whether to produce the horse in different poses, or just one. It was decided that this year the horse would take just one form so it could be said that every artist came out of the same starting gate, and crossed a different finish line.

As for the selection of artists, certain guidelines were issued—no overt commercialism was allowed—but for the most part artists were given a free rein. It was up to sponsors to decide what artist and what design they were willing to underwrite. And to their credit, most of the choices that were made represented the most original, the most clever, the best executed submissions. Perhaps it was because of the pervasiveness of the arts in New Mexico, but there seemed to be an inherent sophistication in the selection process by sponsors.

If one observation were to stand out about the images selected, it would be that the artwork produced in animal

art projects elsewhere—pigs in Cincinnati, fish in New Orleans, Potatoheads in Rhode Island, angels in Los Angeles—seemed to emphasize whimsicality and comedy. While humor was certainly represented in many of the New Mexico designs, the interest on the part of the artists seemed to be in a more serious vein. Artists of all styles and media responded to the opportunity to express their particular artistic sensibilities on the non-traditional canvas of a three-dimensional horse. There were painters, sculptors, photographers and graphic designers. The result was an artistic transformation that was complete, had its own integrity, and was a true one-of-a-kind work of art. Each horse seemed to be a mini-art show in its own right.

In keeping with the narrative tradition of Western art, each horse also had a story to tell.

One of the more interesting aspects that took shape was that even though each horse seemed to be its own breed in the sense that no two horses were alike, distinct herds began to form. You could collect them into different groups —some by artistic style, some by cultural interpretation. The Native American arts community produced stunning and powerful designs which dramatized the special role the horse played in different tribal histories. A New West Herd, showcasing modern interpretations of traditional cowboy themes, appeared. A Contemporary Art Herd, featuring artworks by abstract painters and sculptors, playfully used the horse form as a point of departure for personal explorations.

It was as if a new artform were being created, one that combined folk art and fine art into something dynamic and never seen before. Indeed, the expressive possibilities offered to artists by The Trail of Painted Ponies seemed to renew creative energies throughout the New Mexico art scene.

THE HOME STRETCH

From cave paintings to the Statue of Liberty, public art has enriched human communities in all periods, in every part of the world. When it is placed where it is a part of a community's everyday environment, the experience makes public spaces more welcoming, and at the same time becomes a source of civic pride.

With this in mind, nine New Mexico communities embraced this project and are hosting Painted Ponies. Over one hundred organizations or individuals sponsored ponies. Over one hundred artists painted ponies. Over one hundred different charitable, philanthropic, educational or social organizations will benefit financially when a series of auctions are held at the end of the project. Without each of these groups, all of these people, there would be no project. To everyone involved, we at HorsePower wish to express our sincerest gratitude. They have provided the public with a memorable experience, they have nourished all that the arts do for individuals and society, and appropriately, it is to them that this book is dedicated.

Artist Anne Sawyer puts finishing touches on *Graphics Horse*.

THE HISTORY OF THE HORSE IN THE SOUTHWEST

As the prehistoric sun rose on the "dawn horse" some 50 million years ago, the lineage of our modern-day steed began. Quite unlike today's mount, this little mammal stood no more than 5 hands high. It sported an arched back and raised hindquarters with legs ending in padded feet with multiple hooves.

Although the prehistoric horse is evident in the Old World, the bulk of its evolution took place while foraging the forests and plains of North America and its Southwest. Eventually, various evolutionary branches spread to all parts of the Old World by way of the Bering land bridge and to South America.

The ancestral horse flourished in its homeland until about 10,000 years ago, when it disappeared from North and South America. Scholars speculate that emerging human populations may have hunted the horse into extinction or that devastating diseases eradicated the animal.

Horses would not touch their native soil again until 1519 when Cortés landed at Vera Cruz with 11 stallions, five mares and a foal, destined to conquer the New World and bring the horse home.

After Columbus' first journey, a royal edict required that every subsequent trip to the New World include horses. There is argument over whether they brought the finest stock or common mounts. Some believe they brought the average Spanish horse, likely a hardy Sorraia-Barb cross, to confront a difficult and sometimes deadly journey across the Atlantic. On 30-foot ships shared with men and armaments, the horses faced standing still for three months, rancid food and a mortality rate of 75 to 85 percent. Horses that didn't survive the journey were tossed overboard, and rows of their floating bodies gave rise to the term horse latitudes.

Horses that made it across the sea were resilient survivors. Agile and rugged, they carried conquistadors north through the New World. Coronado entered New Mexico in 1540 and the horse made its reentry into what is now the United States. On his return to Mexico, Coronado's detailed records accounted for all of his horses—whether they died, were killed or returned with him. None were left behind.

It was not until 1598 that the horse again made its home in what is now New Mexico when Oñate came to settle the area. He brought with him soldiers, priests, families and more than 900 horses. In the winter of 1599, as Oñate traveled to Zuni, a vicious storm resulted in the loss of 30 head of horses near Laguna, where tales of wild horses now span generations and train engineers traveling the BNSF tracks point out Wild Horse Mesa.

Aside from lost herds, the old Spanish ways of ranching contributed to the dispersal of the horse from the Rio Grande Valley. Although prized animals were branded and kept close, common horses were turned out on the mesa, captured when needed, and turned back out when the job was done. Thousands of mustangs roamed the countryside under this system.

As history unfolded, the Spanish-Barbs of New Mexico made their mark on a developing nation as they spread through exploration and Indian trading. By the 1700s, populations of the Spanish horse brought up through Mexico stretched from the Carolinas to Florida, west through Tennessee and throughout the western mountains and Great Plains. They became the most common of all horses throughout North America at that time and were highly valued even in non-Spanish areas.

Although standing at just around 14 hands high, they were strong and muscular, fleet and enduring, and their impact on the cultures of New Mexico was beyond compare. Their biggest contribution: mobility.

The horse gave the Spanish the legs on which to conquer a New World. They carried soldiers and priests, explorers and families into New Mexico. Astride their horses, they built communities, hauled in the harvest and marched into battle.

The conquistadors arrived in New Mexico atop beasts the native populations had never seen. A pueblo legend describes the Zunis' first introduction to the horse. Unsure of this strange animal mounted by a soldier of Coronado, a war chief approached the horse and slammed it between the eyes with his fist; chaos ensued. In 1626 a priest wrote of seeing an apache, a general term for the native enemy, outside of Socorro and provided the first record of an Indian on horseback.

When Native Americans adopted the horse, the impact on their culture was enormous. On horseback they could travel two to four times farther in a day and gain an advantage in battle. On the Great Plains they could run with the buffalo. With increased mobility provided by the horse, Native Americans expanded their means of survival.

To white adventurers and settlers, the horse gave the means to push on from the East. It carried the cavalry across the country and pulled families in covered wagons. It was the farmer's tool, the cowboy's companion and the flyer of the Pony Express. And long before the Americas became a prize to be won, the horse influenced the English language with terms like chivalry and cavalier, connoting honor, respect, good manners, and straightforwardness.

There is no way to know the full effect of the horse on our country and our culture, but we can be fairly certain that without it our history and our maps would be altered. With endurance, strength, and tenacity, the horse pressed itself into our world as a partner and a friend.

History even records Cortés' favorite horse, El Morzillo. Inseparably linked, man and horse changed the world—the horse carrying man into the New World and man leading the horse back home

Melissa W. Sais grew up riding horses through the piñon-juniper forests south of Gallup, N.M. Now a writer living in Los Lunas, N.M., she hopes to share the freedom felt on horseback with her own children.

13

Eduardo Fuss, photo

The elite warriors of the Cheyenne were known as "Dog Soldiers" because they frequently fought on horseback, and the Cheyenne word for "horse" translates "big dog." They were the first to arrive at the scene of battle, the last to leave. If they weren't victorious, they fought to the death.

Navajo artist Yellowman specializes in portraits of Dog Soldiers. Here, Yellowman has painted a Cheyenne warrior blessing his horse on one side in a ceremonial expression of gratitude for making him the warrior he is, while on the other he reaches out to stroke his mount in a personal gesture of camaraderie.

Mark Nohl, photo

14

NATIVE AMERICAN PONIES

There was a time when "painted pony" was synonomous with "war horse." Different tribes developed symbols uniquely their own, but the practice of preparing for ceremonial events or forays into enemy territory by painting one's horse with multi-colored symbols was almost universal.

Common too was the application by a warrior of the same colors and designs he put on his own face to his favorite horse, often at the same time. The impact of a fiercely painted warrior on a similarly painted horse was sometimes so dramatic it functioned like an additional weapon, striking fear in an enemy.

Some of the designs represented victorious battles. A hand print told the tale of an enemy slain in hand-to-hand combat. Short horizontal lines stacked on top of one another were coup marks. A hoof track indicated a successful horse raid. Circles around a horse's eyes were believed to improve vision. Lightning bolts were supposed to endow the horse with speed.

Indian war horses told a story. And so do the ponies painted by Native American artists.

When We Were As One
Artist: Yellowman (Navajo)
Sponsor: El Centro Shops and Galleries

Eduardo Fuss, photo

15

Ghost Horse
Artist: Bill Miller
(Stockbridge-Munsee Mohican Nation)
Sponsor: John Garcia

"As a Native American musician and visual artist, I consider my art and my music gifts from my Creator. It was a special challenge to be able to paint on something other than canvas, especially a full-size pony. I believe it brought out a new me. The artistic environment in Santa Fe, the experience of painting in a studio surrounded with other beautifully painted ponies, and the opportunity to "give back" was a surreal and spiritual experience for me. 'May you always ride a painted pony down the Red Road.'"

Eduardo Fuss, photos

16

The Butterfly Horse
Artist: Gregory Lomayesva (Hopi)
Sponsor: Friends of Museum of Indian Arts and Culture

Combining painting with wood sculpture, experimenting with textures and surfaces, and drawing on an irreverent sense of humor as much as his Hopi and Hispanic heritage, this artist used his pony as an opportunity to craft "something really different." And succeeded.

War Pony
Artist: Rance Hood (Comanche)
Sponsor: Rance Hood Gallery

This startlingly realistic recreation of a Comanche war pony reflects the vibrancy and mystical quality of the horses that populate this popular artist's paintings.

Eduardo Fuss, photos

Lightning Bolt Colt
Artist: Dyanne Strongbow (Choctaw)
Sponsor: René Ingold

In Lakota mythology the horse is a Thunder Being who brings storms to Mother Earth. The thunder you hear is the pounding of his hooves. With thunder, lightning and rain come change... and change is like a new day. With this in mind, Native artist Dyanne Strongbow imagined a thunderstorm centered in the horse's hindquarters, breaking up as it moved forward toward his head into the sunny skies of a new day.

Daniel Barsotti, photo

Yesterday, Today and Tomorrow
Artist: Raymond Nordwall (Pawnee/Ojibwe)
Sponsor: The Utz Corporation

Many Native American tribes originally painted on elk and buffalo hides as a form of story-telling. Later they painted on pages from ledger books in a two-dimensional style with no shading or highlighting. This Native artist decided to use the "ledger" style on one side of his horse because it represented "yesterday."

On the other side he painted three warriors on horseback, borrowing the coloration for the horses from the "ledger" style of the past, but rendering them in a more representational manner, which is an example of the contemporary style that many Native artists are using today. This side of the horse represents "today."

His son's handprint represents the "future."

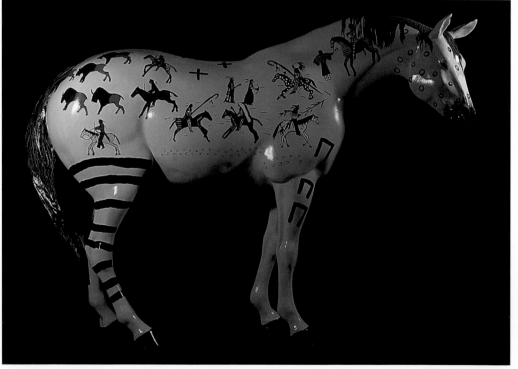

Eduardo Fuss, photo

18

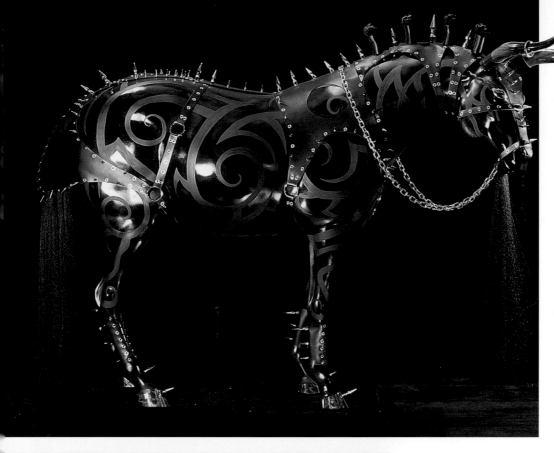

Willing
Artist: Virgil Ortiz (Cochiti)
Sponsor: Friends of the Museum of International Folk Art

Often referred to as one of the most imaginative and compelling artists of his generation, Virgil Ortiz combines Cochiti traditions with personal expression. This black beauty is part pueblo, part demi-monde; tattooed with traditional pottery designs, and leather clad.

Crow Indian War Pony
Artist: Kevin Red Star (Crow)
Sponsor: Zydeco

The setting imagined for his horse by this famous Crow painter is the northern plains of Montana. The horse's right side is decorated with symbols of spirit guardianship. Lightning crashes along the horse's neck. A teepee camp is settled along the horse's flank. Crow ponies wait to run with the buffalo. A Crow mother, "Pretty Shawls", poses with her children: "Winters", the boy, and "Butterfly", the girl. On the horse's rump handprints mark the number of enemies which the rider has counted coup on.

The left side of the horse is male oriented. Four warriors on horseback parade down the neck, returning from a successful raid. (When riders returned from a raid or hunt they would either have their war bonnets on or off, signifying whether they had been successful or not). On the shoulder is the Crow chief "Running Horse" with his full eagle war bonnet. Next to him are two Crow warriors. On the left rump is the Crow medicine man, "Two Rattles".

The horse's spine is intricately adorned with the "Little People." They are the helpers of the Crow. The horse's chest is blessed with the symbol of the "Big Dipper."

The rings around the horse's right eye and left leg are the rider's personal symbols.

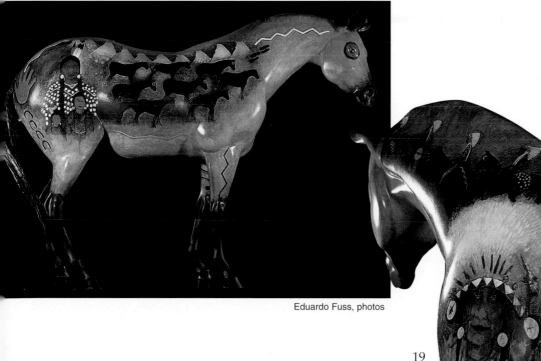

Eduardo Fuss, photos

Tribal Horse

Artist: Jaune Quick-To-See-Smith
(Flathead tribe, Salish nation)
Sponsor: Aguilar Law Offices, P.C.

Work in progress. No photographs available.
An activist/spokesperson for contemporary Native American artists, this artist uses large identifiable Indian icons that have been romanticized by movies and the media as her vocabulary for commenting on the reality of Indian life.

Eduardo Fuss, photo

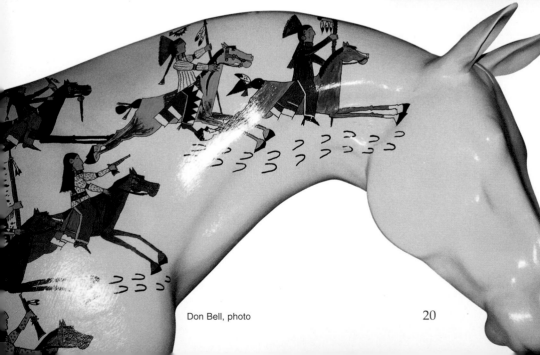

Don Bell, photo

20

Many Horses

Artist: Michael Horse (Zuni)
Sponsor: New Mexico Horse Council

Ledger art represents Native history from the Indian point of view. Power comes through the direct honesty of this art form. It represents a visual way of storytelling, as well.

On one side of "Many Horses," the artist depicts a horse raid. Stealing horses from one another was almost a game between many tribes, while stealing horses from soldiers and white settlers was a way of gaining wealth and honor. On the other side, a war party heads into battle. In keeping with tradition, the small figures that seem to float over the heads of certain warriors signify their name and importance within the tribe.

Hold Your Horses, Mom

Artist: Doug Hyde (Nez Perce)
Sponsor: Community Bank,
The Challenge Group

"The Nez Perce's life revolved around the appaloosa. I pictured a young boy holding his mother's parade horse. He is bored and begins to draw visions in the dirt. His mother calls him, but he replies, 'Hold your horses, Mom.'"

Don Bell, photo

Lowrider (left)

Artist: Ramona Sakiestewa (Hopi)
Sponsor: New Mexico Committee, National
Museum of Women in the Arts

Of Hopi descent, this internationally renowned textile artist wanted her pony to reflect New Mexico's unique culture. "One day I saw a lowrider that had been painted a translucent Monet blue, and I decided to find a body shop that could do something like that for my horse." Painted a candy-apple red with gold flecks scattered across its belly, the horse is adorned with a one-of-a-kind weaving: a saddle blanket resembling a traditional Navajo courting blanket but made from the same lush chenille lowriders use to upholster their vehicles.

Jack Parsons, photo

21

ewAllen Contemporary, photo

Caballitoscope a la Peña

Artist: Amado Peña (Hispanic, descended
from Yacqui Indians on his mother's side)
Sponsors: Dream Catcher Foundation
and Santa Fe Habitat for Humanity

"I grew up around horses, and they have been
an important part of my life. I've ridden them.
I've trained them. I've played with them and
I've been bucked off them a few times. Now
the horse becomes my canvas. Horse and
Artist have become one. No gimmicks, noth-
ing fancy, just horse, paint and my tribute to
the people of the Southwest."

The Swiftness of an Eagle and the Strength of a Bear
Artist: Art Menchengo (Santa Clara Pueblo)
Sponsor: Hyatt Regency Tamaya Resort & Spa

"The coming of the horse changed the way of life for the Plains Indians. With the horse they traveled farther and faster to better hunting grounds. When they rode their horses into battle, they were as one. The horse was a sign of wealth and power. So attached were Indians to their horses that they made songs for their steeds. They also made effigies of their horses if killed in battle. The horses were trained hard, and instilled in them was fearlessness, speed, and stamina. Hence the name: The Swiftness of an Eagle, and the Strength of a Bear."

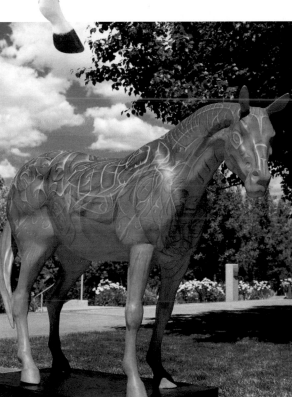

Don Bell, photo

Tlingit Robed Horse
Artist: Clarissa Hudson (Tlingit)
Sponsor: The Santa Fe Rotary Club

The Northwest Coastal style of art is stylized and interpretive. Images overlap, blend into one another, fade away. This Native Inuit artist, famous for her one-of-a-kind ceremonial robes, has incorporated many of the animal designs and motifs used in her robes into an astonishing design that so looks like a wood-carving it begs to be touched. A raven beak turns into the mouth of a dragon that is part of a salmon that flows into the claws of a bear that is an extension of a frog.

Eduardo Fuss, photo

Shelley Heatley, photo

Eduardo Fuss, photo

The Stone Pony
Artist: Denny Haskew (Potawatomi)
Sponsor: John and Chris Harris

"All of life combines in this wonder called the Universe. As the dominant species at the moment, we humans do not always see the connection of one living thing to another living creature.

This 'stone pony' is a small attempt to show that a piece of stone and a horse are both living energies of this universal home."

Don Bell, photo

The Perfect Horse
Artist: Doug Coffin
(Potawatomi and Creek)
Sponsor: The Eldorado Hotel

Wanting to take his pony "a step beyond, rather than use it as a canvas," Native artist Doug Coffin transformed it into an entertainment center, complete with a recessed champagne cooler in its back, a cigar holder cut into its tail, and a new color television inset into its hindquarters.

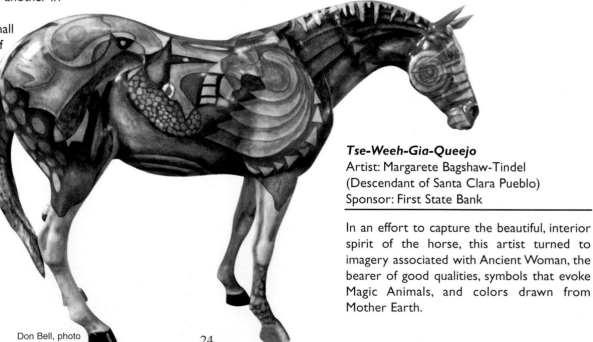

Tse-Weeh-Gia-Queejo
Artist: Margarete Bagshaw-Tindel
(Descendant of Santa Clara Pueblo)
Sponsor: First State Bank

In an effort to capture the beautiful, interior spirit of the horse, this artist turned to imagery associated with Ancient Woman, the bearer of good qualities, symbols that evoke Magic Animals, and colors drawn from Mother Earth.

Don Bell, photo

24

When They Ran With Freedom
Artist: Benjamin Nelson (Navajo)
Sponsor: The La Fonda Hotel

" 'When They Ran With Freedom' represents pre-settled America when Native Americans were able to roam free and were not restricted. In the horse there was a great power and the Native American people were able to bridle that strength. With this power their limits were unfathomable and they could ride to the stars. Through the power of the horse the Indian Nations became strong and united. Native Americans took great pride in their love for their horses as well as their families."

Eduardo Fuss, photo

Pueblo Pony
Artist: Arlo Namingha (Hopi)
Sponsor: Devoted Friends of Gerard's House

Working with the idea of a Paint Horse (Appaloosa), this sculptor wanted to incorporate some aspect of his native culture (Hopi) along with the idea of working various woods into the final product. "I opted to carve symbols relating to the pueblo culture in the circular mahogany pieces I inlaid in the horse. The symbols I used relate to important and necessary meanings not only to my native culture, but also to all cultures and life in general."

Niman Fine Art, photo

Shelley Heatley, photo

Tewa Horse
Artist: Tom Tapia (Tesuque)
Sponsor: The Santa Fe New Mexican

Known for his pottery, painting, and day job as a tribal policeman, this Tewa native has adorned his pony with traditional designs. The sash represents good faith and fortune, the blanket honors the horse as a bold and strong being, the eagle represents good luck, and the handprint stands for the loving touch of all creation.

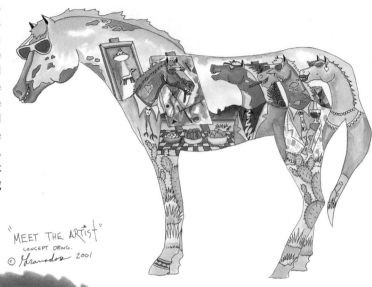

"MEET THE ARTIST"
CONCEPT DRWG.
© Granados 2001

MADCOWpony
Artist: Bernie Granados Jr. (Apache)
Sponsor: Loretto Chapel

Although new to the scene, the humorous, opinionated, happy-go-lucky MADCOWponies have already begun to make a name for themselves in the world of fine art as spokespersons for creatures of all species. On the right side, "Goin' to Pow Wow" depicts the regaled travelers "passin' thru" the sprawling New Mexico landscape. Their excitement and anticipation show through even the coolest shades, man. Cactus candy, hot chili peppers, alfalfa frybread, here we come! On the left side, "Meet the Artist," the MADCOWpony entourage is attending an "al fresco" art exhibit at the rez, and get to meet the creative genius responsible for the unusual body of work.

Don Bell, photo

The Horse from the Four Directions
Artist: David K John (Navajo)
Sponsor: Kiva Fine Art

According to Navajo folkways, the Spaniards did not bring the horse to The People, it came as a gift from the gods. Be that as it may, once the horse was introduced to the Navajo, it not only brought more changes to the old way of life than any other possession ever acquired from the white man, it was adopted into their myths, tales and other legendary lore. This Navajo artist has incorporated the horse's symbolic significance in ceremony into his design.

Don Bell, photo

Blue Medicine
Artist: Mary Iron Eyes
(Osage & Eastern band Cherokee)
Sponsor: David and Judy Standridge

"'Blue Medicine' is not only a piece of art that impacts those who witness it, but it is also an intricate part of expressing healing and support for New Mexico's communities. It is important to acknowledge all the people, children and families who placed their individual hand prints that completed a vision and personal prayer.

May we all remember that we should embrace the highest good for those in need. Art is life and we are fortunate to be able to follow its path. HorsePower New Mexico has been the path for many of us."

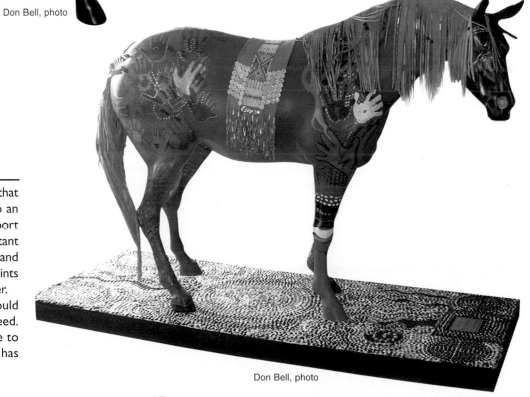

Don Bell, photo

27

THE NEW WEST

The horse has been an inspiration to man since he first attempted to express himself creatively. From Paleolithic painters who drew astonishing equine images on cave walls 15,000 years B.C., to the Renaissance drawings of Leonardo da Vinci, to the abstract paintings of Pablo Picasso, the horse has been a constant muse, and equine imagery has been explored with endless variations. The horse is a symbol of beauty, power, virility, bravery, skill, loyalty, freedom, triumph, wildness. Fantastic equines—the centaur, the unicorn, Pegasus—have appeared in myths and legends.

The artwork generated by The Trail of Painted Ponies updates this time-honored tradition. As inspiring as the project has been to artists and sculptors, it has also stimulated creative efforts in other media. Schoolkids in Espanola wrote poems about their favorite ponies. Carlsbad students painted small plastic horses. An Albuquerque high school ran a horse design competition. The Santa Fe Youth Symphony announced a Young Composer Competition inspired by "Thunderbird Suite," Joel Nakamura's pony. Several filmmakers have created documentary films on the project. And Kay Hilary, a songwriter from Coyote, New Mexico, wrote an original song named *The Trail of Painted Ponies*.

Cowpony
Artist: Lori Musil
Sponsors: Pak Mail, Signs Today, Rio Bravo, Southwest Spanish Craftsmen, Paper Tiger

At first you see a painted horse. Look closer and you see Hereford cows emerging from the shapes and muscles of the horse. Look more closely and you will find a savvy sorrel cowpony hiding amidst the herd of red and whites. This artist loves a good joke and a pun.

Once, while working at a friend's roundup, she was told to catch her mount, a sorrel, only to find this horse gifted at disguising himself in the herd of cattle. She was able to track him down by watching for his pointed, upright ears... a cow's ears stick out sideways. Thus 'Cowpony' was born.

Once she had the idea, then came the challenge of fitting the anatomy of the cattle to that of the horse... a nose to a bulging muscle, the belly of a cow to that of the horse, the face of a cow wrapped over the horse's face. With millions of brushstrokes she brought the cattle to life, as well as the spirit that is "Cowpony."

Eduardo Fuss, photo

Horse Feathers
Artist: Kathy Morrow
Sponsor: Old Town Emporium

Native American influences have been a part of this artist's life since childhood: she was raised on the San Carlos Apache and Pine Ridge Sioux Indian Reservations. Her designs come from legends, reality, friendships and dreams.

With her pony, the white plume of the eagle feather transcends to its dark tip in an array of spots, just as it does in the Appaloosa horse. This unity of design is the perfect background for the painted horses that represent the rainbow of mankind. Black man, Yellow man, Red man and White man race across the patterns of horse and feather to create harmony at its best.

Margaret Pratt photo

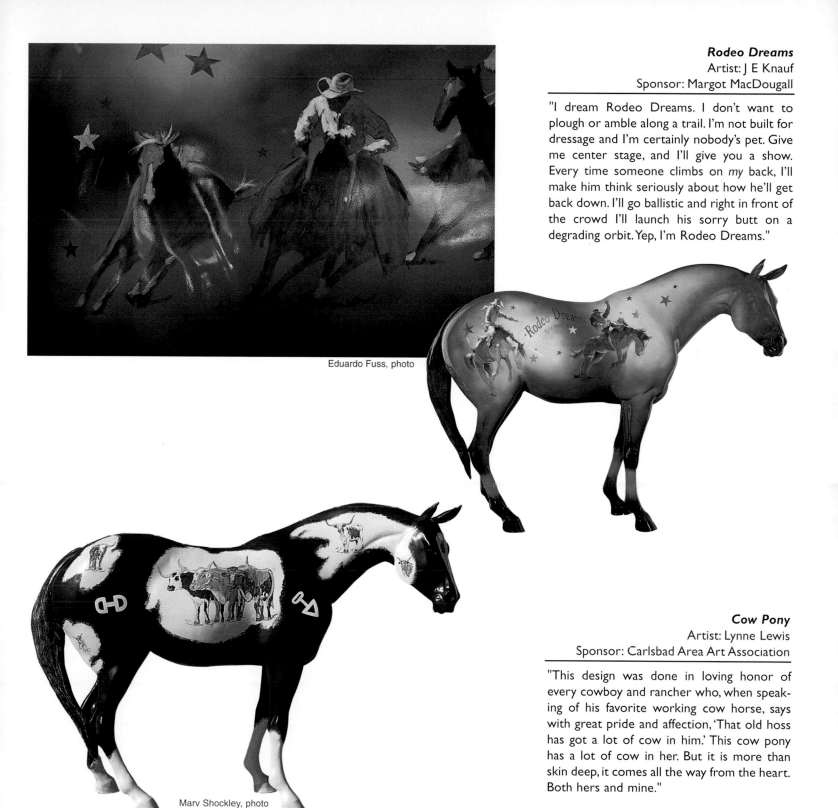

Rodeo Dreams
Artist: J E Knauf
Sponsor: Margot MacDougall

"I dream Rodeo Dreams. I don't want to plough or amble along a trail. I'm not built for dressage and I'm certainly nobody's pet. Give me center stage, and I'll give you a show. Every time someone climbs on *my* back, I'll make him think seriously about how he'll get back down. I'll go ballistic and right in front of the crowd I'll launch his sorry butt on a degrading orbit. Yep, I'm Rodeo Dreams."

Eduardo Fuss, photo

Cow Pony
Artist: Lynne Lewis
Sponsor: Carlsbad Area Art Association

"This design was done in loving honor of every cowboy and rancher who, when speaking of his favorite working cow horse, says with great pride and affection, 'That old hoss has got a lot of cow in him.' This cow pony has a lot of cow in her. But it is more than skin deep, it comes all the way from the heart. Both hers and mine."

Marv Shockley, photo

31

Boot Scootin' Horsey
Artist: Carla Slusher
Sponsor: Century 21
Associated Professionals

"From the moment I heard about 'The Trail of Painted Ponies,' ideas for designs began to flow. At my studio on the ranch in south-eastern New Mexico, I envisioned a horse wearing a cowboy hat, painted on jeans, and color-coordinated boots. A dancing horse ready for a night on the town. The bandana was added at the last moment for balance and color. Upon completion, I stepped back to take a look. At that moment it so happened my favorite country station played a song by Brooks and Dunn. So I cranked up the volume and Boot Scooter and I danced to 'The Boot Scootin' Boogie.'"

Marv Shockley, photo

Bill Manns, photo

Happy Trails
Artist: Nevena Christi
Sponsor: Back At The Ranch

A horse that reflected the style and costumes worn by Gene Autry and Roy Rogers in old Hollywood westerns—'30s and '40s cowboy retro, in other words—was the initial dream of this fine artist and former fashion designer. To give it an edge, she also wanted the horse to look like it was made of tooled leather, with a vintage saddle cinched on its back. The final touch—"I want everything I do artwise to light up"—was to add an electric lariat.

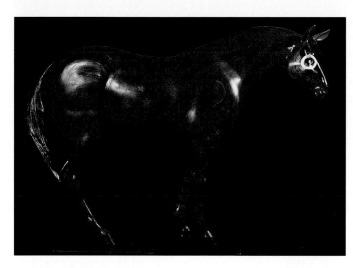

Ceremonial War Horse
Artist: Carole LaRoche
Sponsor: Los Alamos National Bank

"Warrior" is a familiar theme for this artist, so the idea of painting a life-size "warrior horse" was a natural progression. When the time came to actually paint, she tackled the challenge with a large brush, shades of red and a rush of emotion. Once the horse was red, out came the black paint for the symbols, swirls, dots, stars and stripes. Then, the final sign: her hand, dipped in black and pressed on the horse's flank: The artist/warrior mark of ancient cultures.

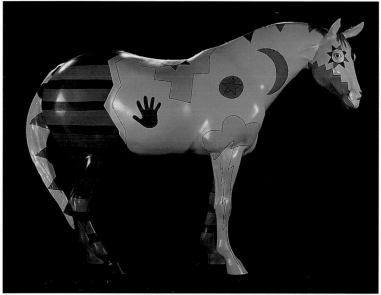

Eduardo Fuss, photos

Spirit War Pony
Artist: Tavlos
Sponsor: Bill and Mary Lynn Oliver

The list of influences this artist credits for influencing his pony begin with an Illinois childhood steeped in the folklore of the Illini Indians, where playing "Cowboys and Indians" was the pastime and his favorite TV programs included The Lone Ranger and Tonto. But even though "Indians" were omnipresent, he never met one and had no idea they were alive, well and prospering until he moved to Santa Fe in 1970 and experienced their culture, history, ceremonies, and fantastic art. "If it can be said that the Plains Warrior and his War Pony were one—each an extension of the other—so it is that my painted pony reflects my art in its entirety."

Eduardo Fuss, photo

Desert Dream Horse
Artist: Ellen Alexander
Sponsor: First National Bank of Santa Fe
and Southwestern College

"Desert Dream Horse came about in a funny way. When I showed my partner, Don Bell, the designs I was planning to submit to Horse-Power, he said, 'They're nice. But I wish you would do a 'doodle horse'. You know, the kind of doodles you sketch when we're driving across country and you get bored. The kind of designs where everything is connected and turns into something else.' So I did that just to amuse him, and that's the one everyone liked."

A Wild Ride Down Memory Lane
Artist: Spencer Kimball
Sponsor: First National Bank of Santa Fe

My idea was to paint a tribute to American pop culture; more specifically, Roy Rogers and Dale Evans, my personal favorites.

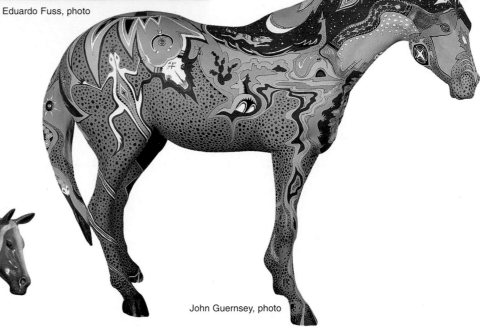

John Guernsey, photo

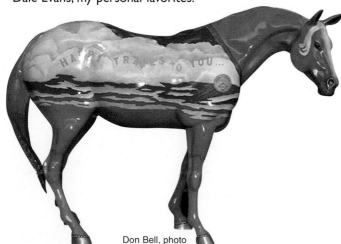

Don Bell, photo

Blondes!
Artist: David DeVary
Sponsor: DeBella Fine Gems and Jewelry

"The 'American Dream' is what I'm trying to capture. Like the more traditional western artist, I'm fascinated with the romantic, idealized western myth. My cowgirls, on either side, and the palomino pony are all very idealized and very blonde! In the use of copper leafing, the images do become more of a symbol. The piece is an icon. The ideal. The super-ordinary."

Dancin' on the Trail
Artist: Michele vandenHuevel
Sponsor:
Sangre de Cristo Communities Interacting

The figures on this pony are floating in the blue New Mexico sky, and dancing in the desert. In the words of the artist, "They represent a celebration of life in an environment of joy."

Blue Night
Artist: Ford Ruthling
Sponsor: Friends of Desert Academy

Photograph unavailable.
Although "Magic Realism" is often used to describe this artist's distinctive style, he prefers the term "Personal" because his work carries the individual stamp of one who has searched for his own methods of representing nature rather than being taught existing techniques.

Horse Apples

Artist: Donna Howell-Sickles
Sponsor: HorsePower New Mexico

"My work frequently deals with women's roles, myths and stories. Horse Apples is a light-hearted take on the standard creation story— a story that has had a huge impact on womens' lives for the past several thousand years. Obviously, this Eve and Adam have been out of the Garden long enough to have discovered denim and the value of a quiet, leisure moment.

"The garden in which they picnic is styled after Henri Rousseau's many lush Garden of Eden paintings from the late 1800's. Rousseau was an untrained painter celebrated for his fresh and immediate paintings of alluring color that created visual meaning beyond the literal and the obvious. The apple in the original story was a symbol for self-knowledge, and in my art the use of an apple frequently shows the unpredictable results of seeking and gaining new understanding. The Adam on Horse Apples has a slight look of doubt on his face

as he accepts yet another apple from Eve's hand. Who knows where this piece of the puzzle will take them? But these unexpected turns in the trail may not be all bad. After all, Adam and Eve are still together."

36

As Long As There Is One

Artist: JD Challenger
Sponsor: Anonymous

Capturing the spirit of Native Americans is this artist's mission. Collectively, his paintings tell the story of a people rich in heritage and tradition; stories sometimes poignant, often angry, but always powerful and demanding to be told. Each portrait speaks its own truth, and the artist considers himself the vessel that paints that truth.

In many of his portrait paintings, JD Challenger will place the face of a warrior against a strong background image in order to set the stage, or convey a message. The setting used in the painting "We The People", for example, is the United States Constitution. Here, the Horse, whose power and spirit is intertwined with the Warrior, forms the backdrop for one of his vintage portraits.

Though he sometimes paints specific tribal people - Apache, Seminole - his goal is to represent all Native Americans, not just one group. And so this warrior, Plains Indian in many respects, is more symbolic than representational.

The title comes from a saying passed along by his Native friends: If one of us survives, we all do. A truth that applies to the animal kingdom as well as the Native American community.

Leslie Cronin, photo

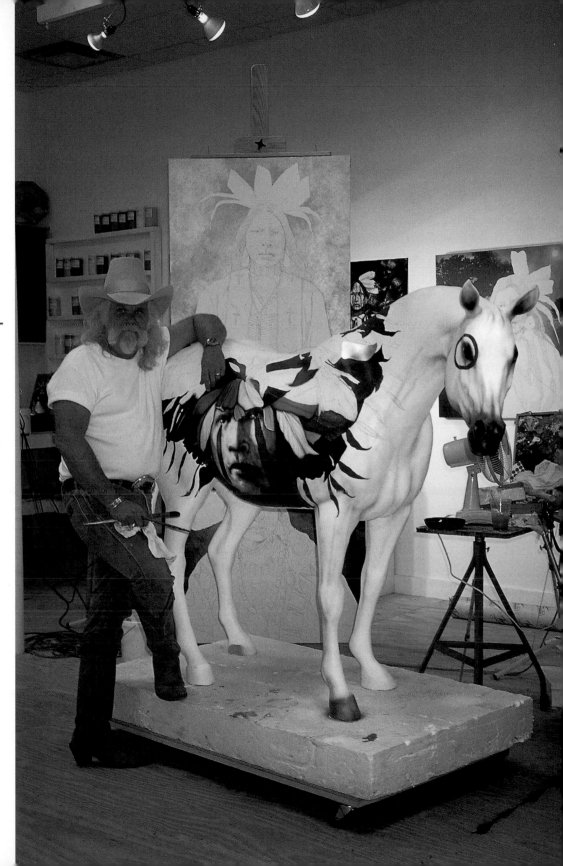

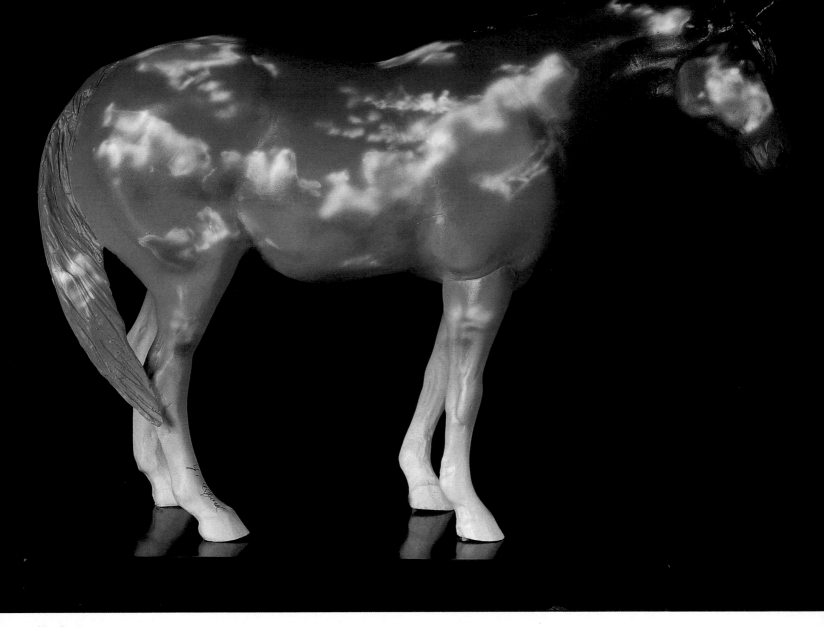

Sky Paint
Artist: Jim Alford
Sponsor: Brother Sun

The skies over the plains and hills of Santa Fe, and the seasonal changes that bring endless varieties of cloud formations and subtle shifts in the quality of light, are of enduring interest to this artist. Masterfully rendered, they become "naturally open windows for metaphysical musing."

EARTH, FIRE AND WATER

It's been said that getting artists to work together on a communal project is like trying to herd cats. Not so, in the case of Carlsbad artists.

An old downtown building that has been redesigned to become the home of both The Artist Gallery and The Carlsbad Education Center for the Arts was converted into a studio for more than a dozen artists who gathered daily to paint their ponies. In that cavernous space, filled with horses, "the noise of stretching and growth and camaraderie could be heard as the artists began to consult, assist, prod and encourage one another," reports Helen Gwinn, one of the artists. "It was common to hear, 'Try red glaze over it,' or 'You'll need opaque white underneath to make the colors vibrate.' Each artist was challenged. Some painted their best work, some painted better than ever before. One actually painted for the first time. Another artist was painting again after a twenty year hiatus. Accompanied by rock music, country music, Garrison Keillor and Rush Limbaugh, they laughed, they joked and the numbers grew."

The Carlsbad Foundation, the city's financial good-fairy, saddled up and aided wanna-be sponsors until, at last count, Carlsbad boasted 21 horses, all underwritten by local merchants, individuals, businesses, and civic groups. And some are waiting in line, hoping yet for a position in HorsePower's corral.

Jeremy the Fish Horse
Artist: Arlene LaDell Hayes
Sponsor: Joe Wade Fine Arts

Merging the conscious and the subconscious while creating work that at times is reminiscent of the 20th Century Surrealistic Movement, Arlene LaDell Hayes's paintings are honed by her own singular vision. They are a kaleidoscope of color, often expressing forms found in dreams, and entice the viewer to take part in the festivities portrayed on the canvas.

Eduardo Fuss, photo

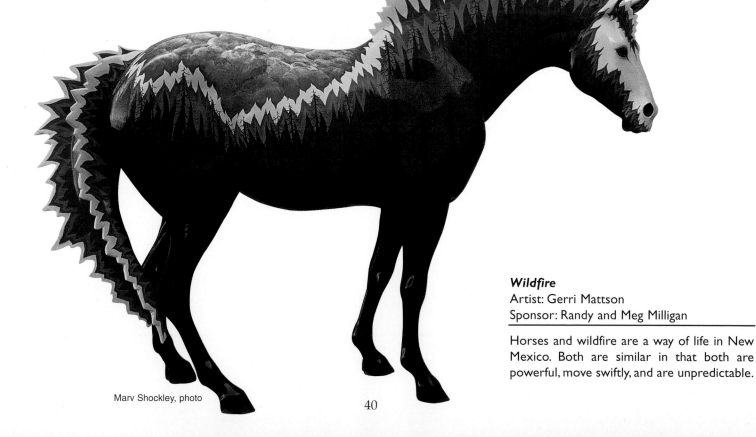

Wildfire
Artist: Gerri Mattson
Sponsor: Randy and Meg Milligan

Horses and wildfire are a way of life in New Mexico. Both are similar in that both are powerful, move swiftly, and are unpredictable.

Marv Shockley, photo

40

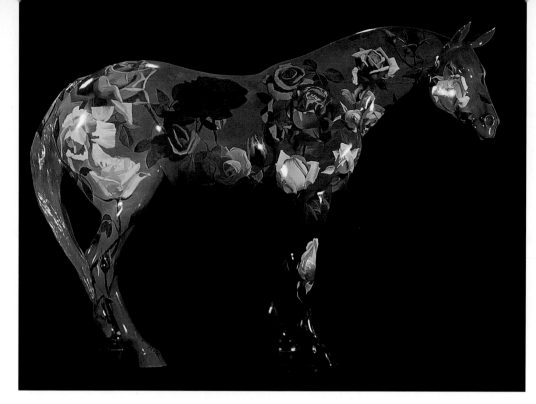

Rosie the Apparoosa
Artist: Marianne Hornbuckle
Sponsor: Santa Fe Youth Symphony

"Apparoosa began life as a computer design: a small rose-covered pony on a sheet of paper. When the life-size pony was delivered to my studio on a cold February day, it was exciting to imagine that blank 3-D surface growing from a sketch to a riotous display of multi-hued roses in bud and bloom, sprouting from earthen hooves and thorny branch-covered legs....

"At first I painted under directional light from overhead, but as the air warmed with spring I opened the doors wide each day so each bud and blossom sprang to life in full sun. Not a single rose was repeated, and the dimensionality created by fully lit blossoms and buds on her graded neutral background gave her a depth I could not have imagined or achieved in a computer design. I dubbed her Rosie, and as she departed her first stable on a warm May day, the three real rose bushes by the studio door bloomed more profusely than any past spring, as if to compliment her radiant and unusual beauty."

Blue Horsizon
Artist: Jim McGarrell
Sponsor: Roswell Museum and Art Center Foundation

"I was thinking in blue," says the artist, who was Artist in Residence at the Roswell Art Museum at the time he painted his pony. "My concept was that of a New Mexican horizon circling the body with a sunrise on one side, a sunset on the other, a day-lit sky above, and a night-time landscape below. Like all my paintings, it is an improvisation based on visual invention rather than direct observation."

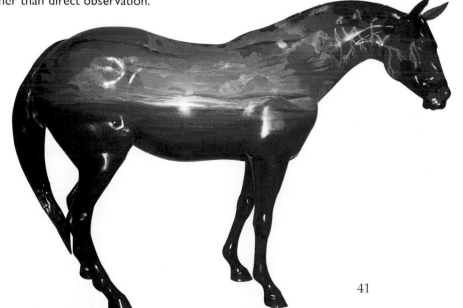

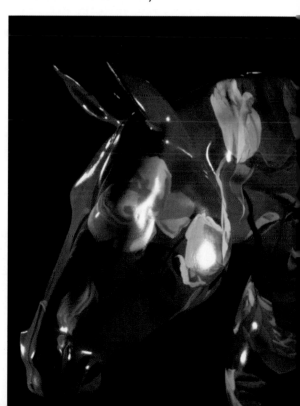

Muy Caliente
Artist: Pat Beason
Sponsor: Girls, Inc. of Sun Country Youth

This horse is hot. Chilis of all shapes, colors and sizes are grown throughout New Mexico. Green, red, yellow, orange, purple—as many varieties of color as there are bands in a rainbow. Put this horse on a track and the rest of the racers would eat her dust.

Marv Shockley, photo

Horse Radish
Artist: Wayne Whiting
Sponsor: Pecos Valley Potter's Guild

It was pointed out to the artist that horseradish is a white root, so why did he use red radishes in his design? His response was that in Central Europe in the 12th century, horseradish was called "meerettich", German for "sea radish" because it grew by the sea. When the use of horseradish spread to England during the Renaissance, the English mispronounced the German "meer" calling it "mareradish." Eventually "mare" was replaced by "horse" and thus horseradish. Considering the history of the term, he felt that a radish by any other name could still end up a horseradish.

42

Spring Filly-ing in the Guadalupe Canyons
Artist: Israel Palma
Sponsor: Carlsbad Arts & Humanities Alliance

The rugged beauty of the Carlsbad Caverns National Park and the Guadalupe Mountains in southeastern New Mexico inspired the "hide painting" on this artist's pony.

Marv Shockley, photo

Eduardo Fuss, photo

Caballo de Jardín
Artist: Gino Miles
Sponsor: The Inn at Loretto

Accustomed to working in three-dimensions, this artist endeavored to do something sculptural rather than painterly with his pony. His use of tin cutouts emulate his abstract fabricated bronze sculptures, while his use of plant materials reference his garden sculptures. The combination, as well as creating interesting contrasts, makes this a distinctively signature work.

El Vado

Artist: Chrissie Orr & Students
Sponsor: Patricia & Charles Senn

The concept for El Vado evolved from a variety of thoughts. The notion that the horse is a symbol of freedom; that it was used as a form of transportation along the ancient trade route from Mexico City, across the Rio Grande, to El Norte and Santa Fe, a route still traveled by those seeking a new life in America. Appropriately, it is decorated with newspaper clippings from local newspapers in New and Old Mexico, symbols that represent water, growth and renewal, and a handprint of Nobel Peace Prize winner Adolfo Perez Esquivel, an activist who seeks "to be a voice for those who have no voice." El Vado translates "a flat, shallow and firm spot in the river, where one can cross by foot, on horseback or in a carriage."

Ghost Ranch Ponyscapes

Artist: Claudia Tammen
Sponsor: Donna Clark

Two views of the spectacular landscape surrounding Ghost Ranch, a conference center in Northern New Mexico, adorn this pony: a view of Pedernal, the sacred site of the Navajo and Apache, and the mountain often painted by Georgia O'Keeffe; and a view of Chiimney Rock, a distinctive sandstone formation and well-known hiking trail.

Sandia Dream

Artist: Ben Levy
Sponsor: Jewish Federation of Albuquerque

The Native American culture indigenous to New Mexico, the fantastic mix of "earth tones" surrounding us, and the historical role of the horse in the Southwest, shape the inspiration for this pony. "Although 'Sandia Dream' is not abstract, distorted, or brightly painted," says the artist, "she represents all the components of history and nature that we are exposed to on a daily basis."

44

Don Bell, photos

Sea Horse
Artist: Grace Knox
Sponsor: Carlsbad Area Art Association

Twenty years ago, this artist retired from the art scene and put up her paint brushes. The challenge of how she would paint a life-size horse brought her back to the studio.

On the way she stopped at the library. "I have no first-hand knowledge of life in the sea... but after a very short period of research, I found such beauty in even the smallest creature and plant, that I wanted to use all of my painting experience and knowledge to capture it in a serious manner."

Visitors dropped by daily, some bringing her shells, photos and stories. But it was the reaction of children that shaped the overall outcome. "I noticed they took a very serious interest in each fish, so I started giving the fish personalities, and giving them a beautiful place to live. I decided against any of the fish that might scare them. They did like the octopus, and did not find it threatening... They would ask why I hadn't added a certain fish, and I would try and work it in to surprise them before their next visit. Adults and children all wanted a turtle, so before I finished I found a nice place in the rocks where he could take his nap."

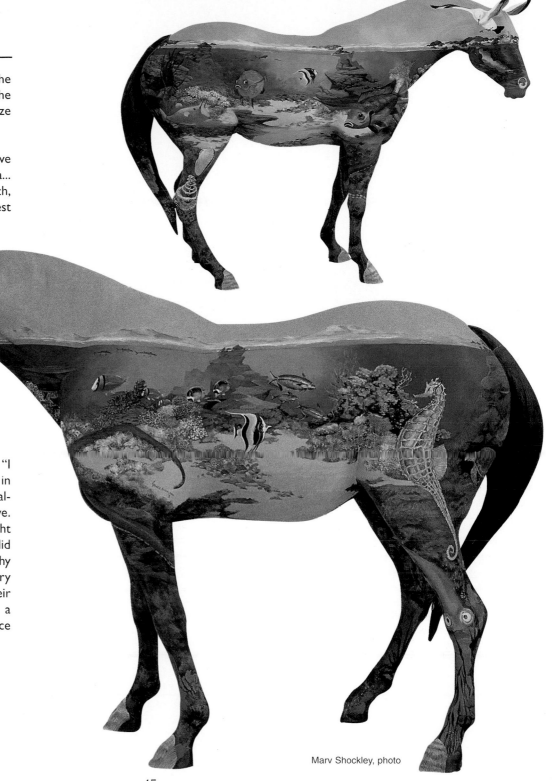

Marv Shockley, photo

45

Jack Parsons, photo

Caballo Brillante
Artist: Roger Montoya
Sponsor: Good Hands Gallery

Some 50 people, ranging in age from 5 to 81, contributed to the making of this horse. First, they trooped out to local dumps that had not been used for twenty years to gather glass bottles and ceramic jugs. Then, under the leadership of Hispanic artist Roger Montoya, the materials were smashed, collected and applied to the surface of the painted pony, forming a kaleidoscopic mosaic surface that has to be seen to be believed. As if that were not enough, "Caballo Brillante" rotates on a solar-powered turning device that captivates viewers with a reflective dance of color and light.

SPANISH BARBS

Despite the Caribbean horse ranches established by the Spanish in the 1500s, the most common route of horses into North America was through Mexico. As explorers established settlements in what is now the Southeast, the Chickasaw, Choctaw and Creek Indians acquired many of the horses. Later, English colonists would mistakenly classify these horses as "native." Seeing their value, they crossed their English racing horses (Oriental Barbs) with the Spanish Barbs, creating the Colonial Short Horse. This type later became known as the American quarter-of-a-mile running horse or the Quarter Horse.

Cultural prejudice caused the Spanish horse's value to be lost on some; as English and French pioneers pushed westward during the 19th century, the horses of Indians and Spanish settlers in western America were considered "foreign" and undesirable for their small size. Herds were slaughtered in efforts to contain Indian tribes and to preserve grazing land for cattle.

Jack Parsons, photo

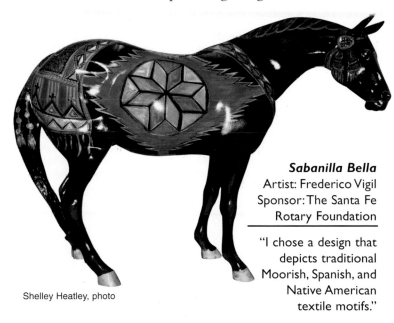

Shelley Heatley, photo

Sabanilla Bella
Artist: Frederico Vigil
Sponsor: The Santa Fe
Rotary Foundation

"I chose a design that depicts traditional Moorish, Spanish, and Native American textile motifs."

Anasazi Spirit Horse
Artist: Robert Rivera
Sponsor: Private Sponsor

While this horse is decorated with designs found on Anasazi pottery that dates back 900 to 1200 years, the fact is the Spanish had not yet arrived on these shores when the Anasazi culture flourished. While painting, the artist found himself thinking about the logs that were hauled by hand from the timbered mountains hundreds of miles away to build the structures at Chaco Canyon, the heart of the Anasazi culture. As he painted he toyed with an alternative title: "Where Were You When We Needed You."

Eduardo Fuss, photo

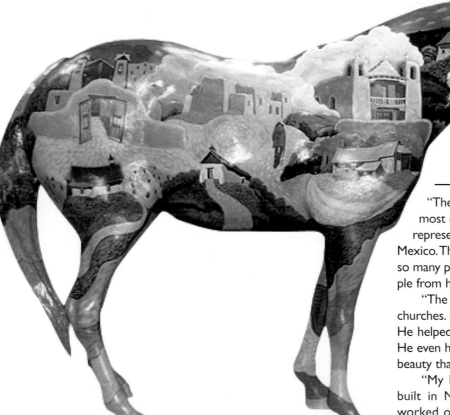

Don Bell, photo

Sacred Heart
Artist: Ed Sandoval
Sponsor: Private Sponsor

"The idea for my horse came to me one night in my dreams - I do most of my thinking in my sleep. I wanted to do something that was representative of my work, that also expressed Northern New Mexico. The idea of old churches was the perfect theme simply because so many people come here to see the old adobe churches. Also, the people from here have a special place in their hearts for the old churches,

"The horse was a big contributor in the building of the old adobe churches. He transported building materials, vigas, adobes, lumber, rocks. He helped to lift heavy timbers to locations on the walls of the church. He even helped to mix the mud in making adobes. We cannot forget the beauty that this animal has given us.

"My horse has a heart painted on his chest. The newer church built in Nambe after the fire in the 30's was a church my father worked on as a young man. All the village people had their quota of adobes they were to make for the new church and deliver to the church site. The church was named 'Sacred Heart.' So is my pony."

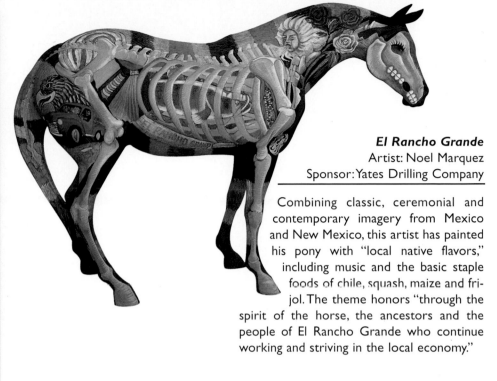

El Rancho Grande
Artist: Noel Marquez
Sponsor: Yates Drilling Company

Combining classic, ceremonial and contemporary imagery from Mexico and New Mexico, this artist has painted his pony with "local native flavors," including music and the basic staple foods of chile, squash, maize and frijol. The theme honors "through the spirit of the horse, the ancestors and the people of El Rancho Grande who continue working and striving in the local economy."

José Rivera, photo

War Horse
Artists: Luis, Adan and Orion Jimenez
Sponsor: Michael and Jeanelle McGuire

When his two teenage sons appealed to this famous sculptor to become involved in the Painted Pony project, he agreed under two conditions: the imagery had to have social content; and it would have to be a collaborative effort among the three of them. After several family discussions, they decided on the concept of a "War Horse." But rather than a glamorized version of an Indian war pony, they wanted to create something "people were not aware of, but would start thinking about." Thus, a horse that represented "how connected, through history, New Mexico has been to the military-industrial complex. From the Indian Wars to wars with Mexico to military bases to bombing ranges to Trinity, where the first atomic bomb was tested, this state has an intimate connection with War."

With its tail and ears trimmed, and glowing red light bulbs set in the eye-sockets, the pony has taken on the symbolically skull-like look of a death figure that the artists wanted.

"Just another evening ride through the New Mexico desert... Golden sunsets, burning red skies at dusk, the land coming alive as the evening shadows approach... I was sitting in solitude when in one split-second... the living desert had a new cohabitant... There stood vividly before me my Pump Jack Pony amidst the rest of the night creatures... coming to life as the desert quickly cooled down into darkness... an enchanting moment."

Pump Jack Pony
Artist: Judy Norman
Sponsor: Friends of the Assistance League

HORSE COUNTRY

Horses hold a special place in the hearts of New Mexicans, as well as in the state's history.

The first horse race ever recorded historically on American soil was near Bernalillo, New Mexico in 1541. It was a race between Francisco Vasquez de Coronado and one of his men, Rodrigo de Maldonado. Coronado's horse stumbled and fell, injuring him, and he never recovered.

According to the Guinness Book of World Records, the "Most Valuable Horse of All Time" was New Easy Jet, a stud horse from the Buena Suerte Ranch in Roswell. Easy Jet was syndicated for $30 million when his owners made a corporation out of him and sold 50 shares of breeding rights at $600,000 apiece.

Every two years, Albuquerque hosts the U.S. National Arabian Championship Horse Show, which features 97 events, including riding, reining and general appearance.

The world's richest quarter-horse race is the $2.5 million All American Futurity held at Ruidoso Downs.

Add to this the number of horse clubs and associations, training facilities, dude ranches, therapeutic riding programs, rodeos and horse-related events, and you get an idea why so many New Mexico artists find horses an inspiration for their art.

Caballo de Ojos
Artist: Anne Strait
Sponsor: Friends of the Living Desert

This horse was inspired by the brightly colored yarn "God's eyes" that many of us made as children. Ojos are talismans of good luck made by Indians of the Southwest and New Mexico.

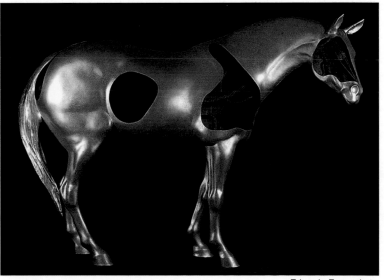

Les Crétoises
Artist: Pascal
Sponsor: Expressions in Fine Art

"I have created this sculpture as homage to the Eternal Feminine, and as a tribute to ancient Crete which was a matriarchal society. There is also some of the theme of the Trojan Horse: within the body of masculine techno-society the nearly hidden female forms are a mysterious and potentially revolutionary presence."

Eduardo Fuss, photo

Taos NEIGHbors
Artist: Valerie Graves
Sponsor: The Historic Taos Inn

Being an artist and raising and showing fine horses came together naturally in this project, according to Valerie Graves. Her pony stands painted with Winter quiet time at the Taos Pueblo on one side, and Hispanic Neighbors raking hay and herding cattle in green summer on the other. The clear blue New Mexico sky and Taos Mountain with its many shadows rises over both scenes.

Barnyard Pony
Artist: Helen Gwinn
Sponsor: Carlsbad Foundation

"My childhood had but one memorable horse: the one I saw only once a year when I visited my grandparents. That horse was like a pet, he lived in the barnyard where my uncle milked the cow, where Granny and I gathered the eggs and where the dog pestered the cat! The other beloved animals lived there too where PawPaw stored the hay for the long winter and parked the tractor at the end of the day. He whistled, the pig snorted, and the swallow swooped. It was my place to catch ladybugs, chase butterflies and plant sunflowers. It was my place to gather thimbleflowers, sing with the robin, and march with the ducks."

Eduardo Fuss, photo

Don Bell, photo

The Enchanted Pony
Artist: Eugene Kimura, Teacher, Jessica Sousa, Student Designer, Painted by Rio Rancho High School Art Academy students Richard Crisman, Alyce Ramos & James Makin
Sponsor: NMEFCU

The design was produced by a student from Rio Rancho High School Art Academy. The execution was accomplished by her art teacher, assisted by several other students. The result is quintessentially Albuquerque, with a Zia-like sunrise bursting gloriously above a jagged horizon, and brilliant hot air balloons drifting lazily over mesas dotted with ancient Indian dwellings.

Route 66 Horse
Artist: Ellen Sokoloff
Sponsor: The Gulfstream Group

Childhood memories of western trips along historic Route 66 imprinted images of diners, motels, gas stations and tourist attractions, which later became part of Americana painter Ellen Sokoloff's artistic repertoire. Her paintings, in her words, "represent a time in our country before franchises took over and closed down many of the 'Mom and Pop' family-owned businesses. A time when there was comfort food in friendly eating establishments and homey motels beckoning the tourist to stay awhile. The highways welcomed a slower pace and folks could stop and rest in friendly conversation. I hope to continue to capture this picture as it disappears under the forceful swing of the wrecking ball."

Daniel Barsotti, photo

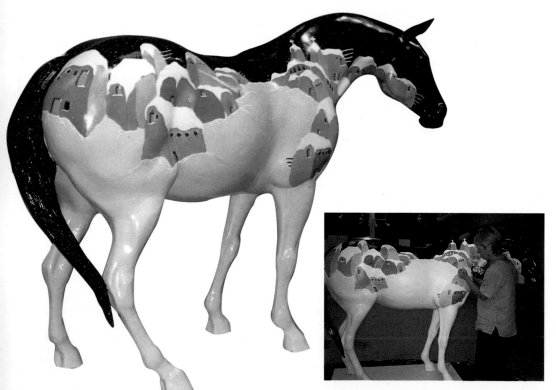

Snow Pony
Artist: BJ Briner
Sponsor: BCA Medical Associates

"I can't imagine a more timeless, endearing image of New Mexico than snow-laden land and an adobe village under a blanket of stars. I began my embellishment by letting the horse dictate, through its contour of muscle and bone, where the valleys of snow, the shape of the village and placement of the adobe homes would exist. It was fitting that the night sky cover the horse like a blanket and run down its tail, lingering like a cold northwest breeze waiting for instructions from the new dawn."

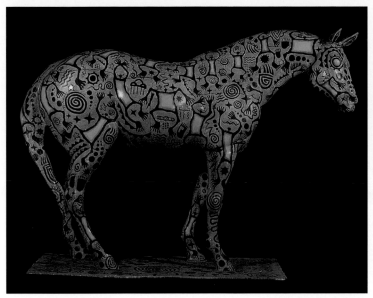

Eduardo Fuss, photo

Anasazi Diaries
Artist: Ty Anderle
Sponsor: Friends of Desert Academy

"This was an adventure in painting in which my original idea of incorporating the images of the prehistoric people of Northern New Mexico—the stories told on the rocks and in the canyons of our area—became something much more. How to use the form of the horse as a canvas was the first challenge. But the deeper I got into the project, the less I saw of the horse and the more I saw of just a wonderful surface to paint on and cover with texture and design. The horse form began to flatten out. The outline was still there, but as a background to be filled in with hundreds of figures and designs. An overall textural pattern developed, one that changed depending on where I stood, but from any perspective was one big three-dimensional canvas. It didn't matter whether or not it was a horse that had been painted.

"But then, something happened. As I was nearing the final stages of painting, all of a sudden the shape and contours of the form emerged in a way that made the horse itself reappear!"

Tracker
Artist: Daniel Morper
Sponsor: Santa Fe Southern Railway

This artist switched from painting landscapes to railroad scenes because trains, he felt, "added a human and an emotional dimension to a landscape," as well as a sense of journey, of coming from and going to new places, and the personal discovery that often comes with travel.

Just looking down the set of tracks, disappearing into a horizon, that he has painted on one side of his pony takes us on a trip.

As he was painting, the artist recognized a parallel between horses and trains, beyond the fact that trains were once referred to as Iron Horses. "Horses represent freedom. They are often portrayed in a field or galloping across a prairie. A train cutting across the wide open spaces evokes a similar feeling, one we also associate with the West."

Eduardo Fuss, photos

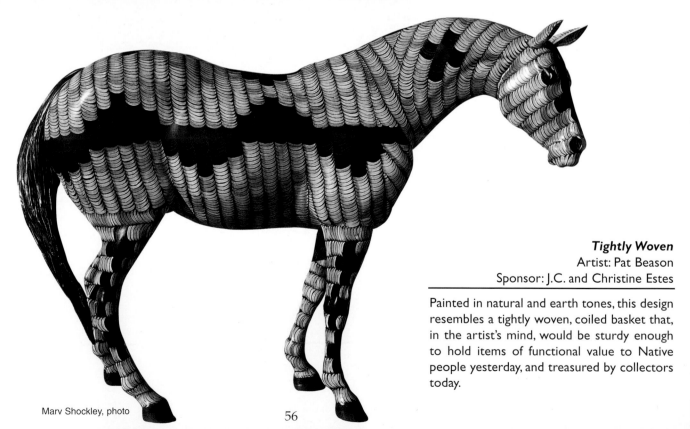

Tightly Woven
Artist: Pat Beason
Sponsor: J.C. and Christine Estes

Painted in natural and earth tones, this design resembles a tightly woven, coiled basket that, in the artist's mind, would be sturdy enough to hold items of functional value to Native people yesterday, and treasured by collectors today.

Marv Shockley, photo

Secretariat

Artist: Christine Picavet
Sponsor: Kathleen Sullivan

Twice, when Secretariat was alive, this artist painted his portrait. So it was only natural that she chose to "recreate" him at the height of his glory: standing in the winner's circle after winning the Kentucky Derby in 1973.

Don Bell, photo

Peaceful Spirit

Artist: Pat Beason
Sponsors: Brantley Farms, E.M. Murphy, D&D Reese, F&C Tracy

The desert landscapes of New Mexico are a welcome getaway from the bustle and hustle of the city. Beneath serene blue skies and fluffy clouds, two Indian women wearing colorful blankets talk about their handcrafted pottery—a conversation that could have taken place hundreds of years ago, as well as today.

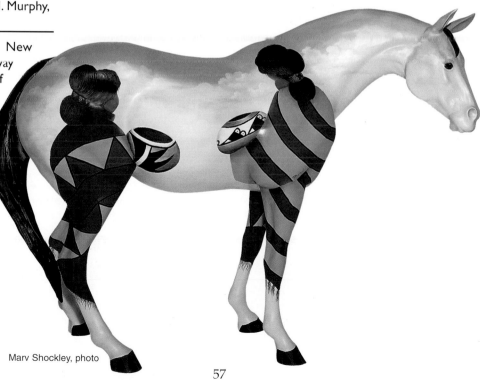

Marv Shockley, photo

57

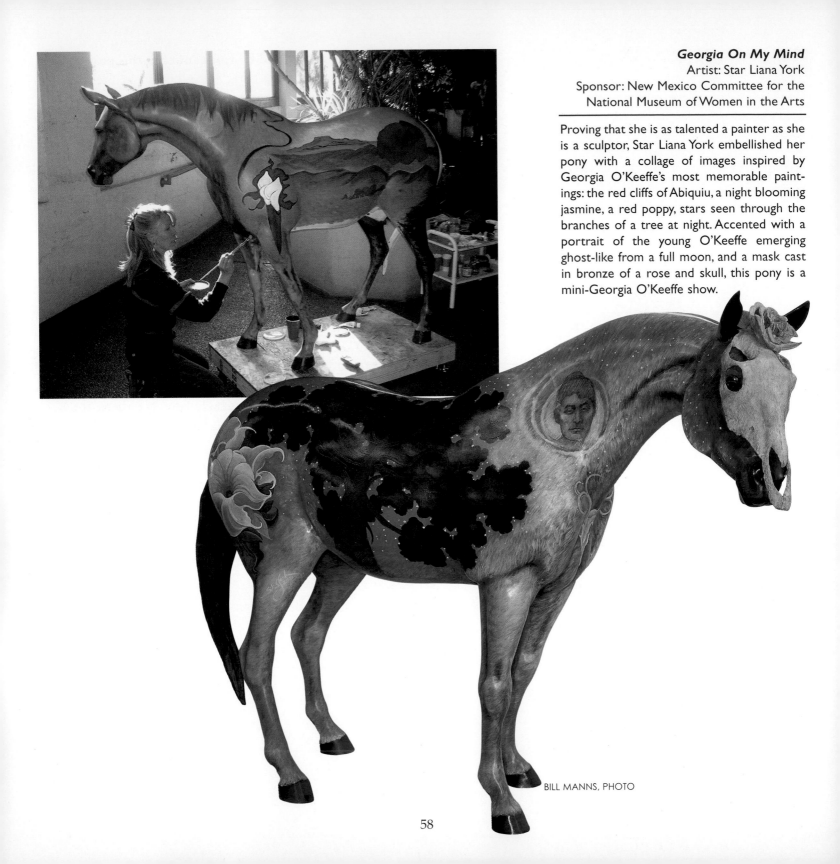

Georgia On My Mind
Artist: Star Liana York
Sponsor: New Mexico Committee for the
National Museum of Women in the Arts

Proving that she is as talented a painter as she is a sculptor, Star Liana York embellished her pony with a collage of images inspired by Georgia O'Keeffe's most memorable paintings: the red cliffs of Abiquiu, a night blooming jasmine, a red poppy, stars seen through the branches of a tree at night. Accented with a portrait of the young O'Keeffe emerging ghost-like from a full moon, and a mask cast in bronze of a rose and skull, this pony is a mini-Georgia O'Keeffe show.

BILL MANNS, PHOTO

58

The equine image used by HorsePower in this project was created by Star Liana York. Star is one of the premiere bronze sculptors working today. She exhibits in galleries across the country, and her work is part of both private and public collections. She has won numerous awards and was featured in a PBS documentary on Artists of the Southwest. When Southwest Art magazine selected 30 artists that had shaped the magazine and the western art market in the last 30 years, Star York was among those chosen.

Her renderings of horses span from prehistory to the present. They include personal interpretations of horses drawn by Paleolithic cave painters, a series based on Leonardo Da Vinci's war horses, as well as depictions of the quarter horses she raises and trains on her 40-acre ranch in Abiquiu, New Mexico, less than ten miles from where Georgia O'keeffe lived.

Created exclusively for HorsePower, her horse form received this tribute from painter John Nieto. "I like this horse. The anatomy is correct. There's body language there. It speaks of the Southwest. If it was running it would be hard to control. It would already have its own power. The way it was done is an invitation. It says, 'Paint me.' Star put her ego aside and created something that works for others. That was smart of her. She did a good job. It's an easy vehicle for a painter to jump on and ride."

Eduardo Fuss, photo

New Mexico Sun Magic
Artist: Storm Townsend
Sponsor: John and Marjorie Wyckoff

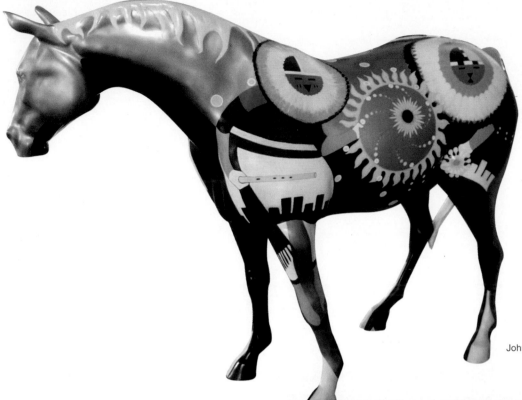

"It was because of the glorious, year-long sun-bright days that we are blessed with in this state, even through frigid winters, that I chose to make New Mexico my home. This horse is my 'Thank you' to the 'Land of Enchantment.' A perfect living symbol is the Palomino horse, here richly embellished with four red sun kachinas dancing with a sunflower sun-disc spinning sun-spots—all complimented with the deep, cool, purple undershadow."

John Wyckoff, photo

Memories of New Mexico
Artist: Charles Azbell
Sponsor: Charles Azbell Gallery

Crimson clouds that dance in fiery, magical hues above the New Mexico landscape. Old pots that don't need a voice to tell of traditions, innocence and hardship. Native American figures rendered in poses and with expressions that seem to symbolize this land and the cultures that call it home. These are the images this artist is known for, and that make up memories of New Mexico.

Run for the Roses
Artist: Dorothy Grandjean
Sponsor: The Grandjean Boys,
In Memory of their Father

"Covering a horse with a calming blanket of roses was symbolic for me, as I've never overcome my fear of horses."

Marv Shockley, photo

Pony Tales
Artist: Fran Larsen
Sponsor: Gallery A

"I want to involve the viewer by taking him on a visual trip through the country I love—Northern New Mexico. 'Pony Tales' presents the story of trips I have taken, and the white road that wanders through the 'painting' is meant to transport the viewer visually, as he walks around the pony, to discover the landscape as it is revealed when night turns to day."

Eduardo Fuss, photo

61

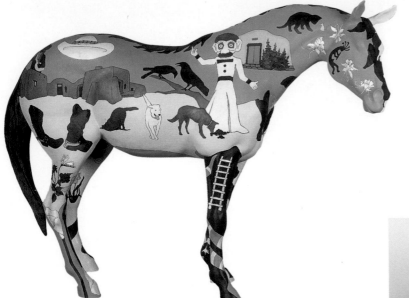

Petroglyph Pony
Artist: Loran Creech
Sponsor: Carlsbad Area Art Association

The mystery behind ancient petroglyphs has always intrigued this artist. And like the horse, petroglyphs seemed synonomous with Native Americans. Painting his pony to resemble the weathered, textured and fissured sandstone that formed the writing tablets of the Ancient Ones, and then incorporating designs found on the rocks in his region, seemed like a natural way to paint a pony.

Graphics Horse
John Guernsey, photo

Artist: Anne Sawyer
Sponsor: Graphics House Gallery

Using crimson, snow and turquoise colors—the red, white and blues of New Mexico—this artist has incorporated many of the icons of the Santa Fe arts scene, the New Mexico landscape, and details of life on her Abiquiu ranch, into her painted pony.

Horse Feathers
Artist: Loran Creech
Sponsor: Chaves County Crime Stoppers

'Horse Feathers' was a term the artist heard often as a child, usually from an exasperated adult. When it came to rendering the term visually on a horse, a blanket Appaloosa, adorned with markings and feathers, came to mind.

Horsienda
Artist: Pat Beason
Sponsor: Denton-Funchess Funeral Home

Quaint and charming, crumbling adobe buildings can be found across the state, like relics of a previous civilization. Applying texture to simulate exposed adobe bricks, and adding vigas to support the ristras of hanging chilis and a traditional ladder, "Horsienda" is a tribute to those who literally built their homes from the ground up.

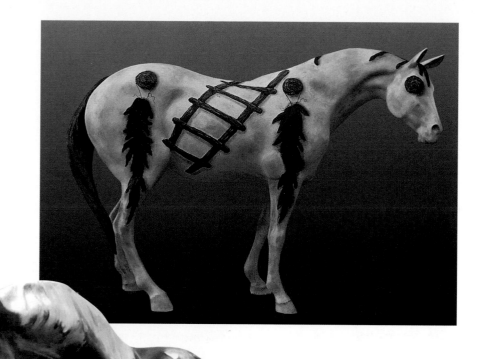

The Roswell Incident (below)
Artist: Mona Slayton
Sponsor: Paul and Patricia Slayton

A Roswell native, this artist grew up on stories about alien spacecraft and government cover-ups. Incorporating "news" about what happened and the speculations that have flourished since "the crash" into a collage that covers her horse, and altering the eyes and mane to promote the "alien idea," allowed her to make a personal statement about The Roswell Incident.

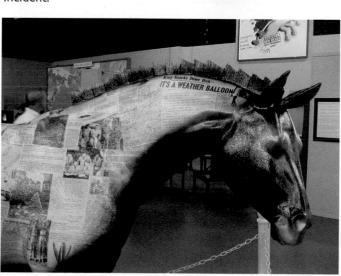

Extraterrestrial Equine (left)
Artist: Dorothy Peterson
Sponsor: Strata Production Company

This horse acknowledges the UFO phenomenon in Roswell. It also speaks to our awareness of vast space in the night sky, when you look up and feel you can almost touch the stars, even though they are light years out of reach. While painting her pony, the artist came to call her "Princess Leia" because she was out of this world.

"My initial incentive to work on this wonderful project was not only the challenge of applying my work to an unusual format, but also to take the opportunity to give back to the community. The bonus came when an unexpected personal journey of recall and reflection of the 'horse days' of my youth came back to me. The solitude of sanding and painting this cast horse opened my thoughts to those days of moonlight rides, endless hours of practice before a big show, as well as daily care of this powerful animal that had lovingly become my best friend over the years. For me, the real power of this fabulous creature came not from its physical size and strength but from its expressive silence, its enduring loyalty and its immeasurable spirit for life. Over time, I had forgotten about some of the wisdom I had learned from my friend. This project whispered reminders that I had been given a great gift that couldn't be lost or broken, but one that was still somewhere deep inside me. It was inspiring and comforting to once again take that journey with my spirit guide of long ago."

HORSEPLAY

Even though we can never know for sure, can only guess what's going on in the minds of animals, domesticated and wild, certain painters, sculptors, photographers have an uncanny capacity to capture animals in a portraiture so revealing that, for a riveting moment, we think we've been let inside.

With many of the Painted Ponies, it's all about character and personality. Some are intentionally ornamental. Others defy explanation. They are just endlessly fascinating to look at. And look at again.

With this herd, viewers should take their own direction and let their imagination come into play, just as the artists have.

Tasty Frieze
Artist: Dianne Schlies
Sponsor: Peg Nelson

In 1999, the actor, producer and director, Ed Harris, hired this Albuquerque artist to reproduce paintings for the Academy Award winning movie, *Pollock*. The movie credit brought her much publicity, which caught the eye of her sponsor. After numerous meetings, they agreed on several designs which emulated Jackson Pollock's style and palette, and the process began.

Says the artist, "Working like Pollock was largely about color, follow-through, and improvisation. It's like jazz, which was Pollock's favorite music, and mine. In that way, it's perfect that the New Mexico Jazz Workshop is the beneficiary of this pony."

(Opposite)
Three Ring Circus Pony
Artist: Kathleen Kinkopf
Sponsor: Korinsky Art Glass & Jewelry

Shelley Heatley, photo

The Southwestern deserts were once ocean bottoms. Where horses ride today, fish once swam. Geological history is fancifully combined with humor to make art in this piece.

Marv Shockley, photo

Horse 'n Buggy
Artist: Bonnie Nelson
Sponsor: Merland, Inc.

The desire to make a play on words and, at the same time, to create a design that compelled the viewer to linger over her pony, led this artist to cover her horse with her favorite creepy crawlies.

The Harley Horse
(Photograph Unavailable)
Artist: David Losoya
Sponsor: Yates Petroleum Corp.

A second-generation lover and owner of Harley Davidson motorcycles, this artist says, "If I was a biker in the 19th Century, this is what I would ride." With the help of friends and family members, Losoya is molding many parts of real motorcycles onto his horse, including mufflers, a taillight and a kick-starter, chains instead of reins, saddlebags, leathers and other elements of horse and bike.

Eduardo Fuss, photo

Eduardo Fuss, photo

**El Diablo and his Friend, Sonny Boy,
From the Garden of Eaten: Fact or
Fiction?**
Artist: Tavlos
Sponsor: Galisteo Home Furnishings

The image and title of this horse came to the artist in one of those dreams that leave a vivid visual impression, but don't make a lot of sense. As the creator of the famous howling coyote wearing a bandana—or infamous, depending on your point of view—the artist hints at several possible interpretations when he asks, "Doesn't every horse project/ ranch house have a Diablo?" As for the snake, "Don't ask me, ask Sonny Boy, he's got all the answers."

Horse Cents
Artist: Loran Creech
Sponsor: Joyce and Donald Manke

For this artist, converting the term "horse sense" into "horse cents" immediately produced a mental picture of a life-size "piggy bank horse" brimming with coins. Simple enough in concept, the execution became more complicated when he tried to depict how pennies would lay and stack in a jar.

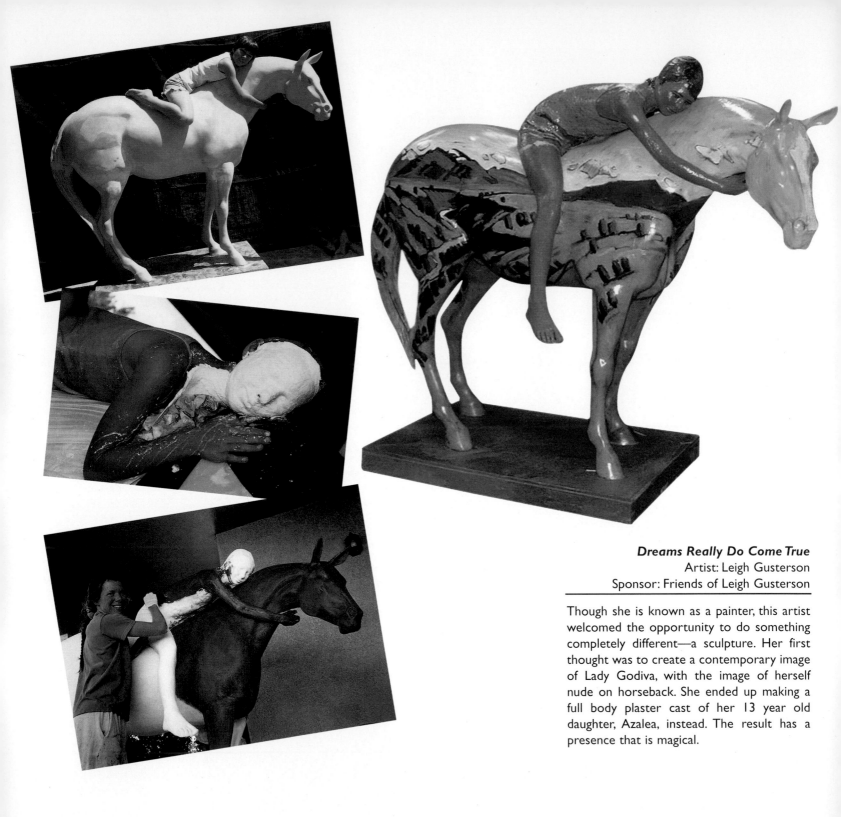

Dreams Really Do Come True
Artist: Leigh Gusterson
Sponsor: Friends of Leigh Gusterson

Though she is known as a painter, this artist welcomed the opportunity to do something completely different—a sculpture. Her first thought was to create a contemporary image of Lady Godiva, with the image of herself nude on horseback. She ended up making a full body plaster cast of her 13 year old daughter, Azalea, instead. The result has a presence that is magical.

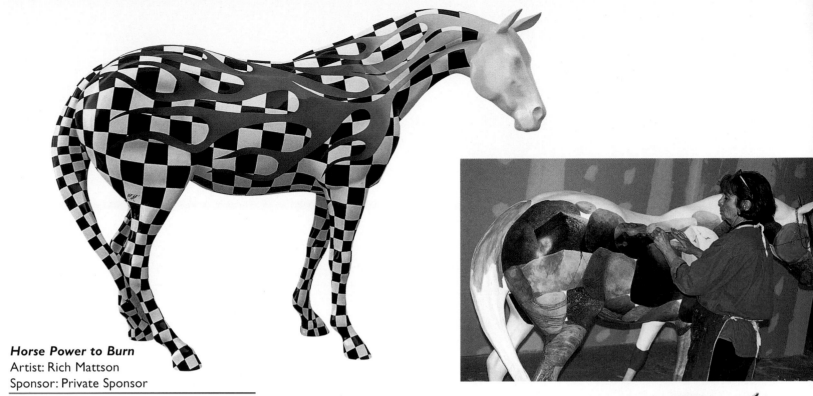

Horse Power to Burn
Artist: Rich Mattson
Sponsor: Private Sponsor

It was the Fifties. Hotrods and drag racing were "in." This artist's older brother was heavy into the cool car scene. Too young to drive, the "sensitive one" thumbed through the hotrod magazines and drew pictures. Exhaust flames. Checkered flags. Asphalt. Those early sketches formed the imagery he would incorporate into his painted pony almost a half-century later.

Rocking Horse
Artist: Helen Gwinn
Sponsors: Frances Feezer,
Claiborne & Russ Power

"Solid, steadfast, tough, unwavering, firm foundation, rugged beauty, constancy... rocks have symbolized all these and more in my paintings. Have I painted rocks! I've painted desert rocks, river rocks, cliff rocks, and petroglyphs. So why not a rock horse?

It was the obvious choice of imagery when I decided to paint on a horse. Rocks on a horse, rock horse, rocking horse. Of course!"

Eduardo Fuss, photo

69

Horse Power
Artist: Shawn Smith
Sponsor: Gateway Christian School

Incorporating "metallic imagery" in a way that gave his horse a "man-made" feeling was the intent behind this pony.

Eduardo Fuss, photo

The Reunion of the Family of Man
Artist: Cal Peacock
Sponsor: Painted Pinto Farms

About her "Medicine Horse" series, of which her painted pony is a part, the artist writes, "It is my intention that these horses go out into the world bearing offerings of beauty and inspiration. They are talismanic reminders of the grace of life's tribulations, so that rather than dragging our past around like an anchor of shame-based victim stories, we might take heart and think of our battle scars with pride, like a badge of courage or credential for the dignity of our character... May these horses take your spirit on a soaring ride to the confluence of what is so—and bring you back a connoisseur, a veteran of beauty."

The movie "Yankee Doodle Dandy," about the life of George M. Cohan and starring James Cagney, was this artist's favorite musical during her teen years. Years later, research revealed to her that the English had their own version of Yankee Doodle Dandy, and it was a laughing matter that referred to a group of young English aristocratic men who had traveled to Italy and picked up the fancy ways of Italians, and upon their return formed "The Macaroni Club." Made fun of, soon they were called Yankee Doodle Dandies, from which came the line in the song, "Yankee Doodle went to town, riding on a pony. Stuck a feather in his cap and called it macaroni."

Thus, 1) the American flag and colorful background from the musical. 2) The Spirit of '76 painting, marching into war to the tune of Yankee Doodle Dandy. 3) Captain Washington on his white stallion. 4) The dancing figures... "mind the music and the step and with the girls be handy." 5) Yankee Doodle Dandy himself, riding into town, on a pony, in his fancy clothes and feather in his cap, the little boys on their stick horses, with their large hats and big feathers, and the town women laughing at him.

Marv Shockley, photo

Stabat Mater
Artist: Harold Joe Waldrum
Sponsor: Red River Ventures

Stabat Mater is Latin for Standing Mother. The first Stabat Mater was Mary standing at the foot of the cross. The concept stands for any mother who grieves for something precious lost. This Stabat Mater stands for all the mothers who have lost a child to the horror of AIDS.

Don Bell, photo

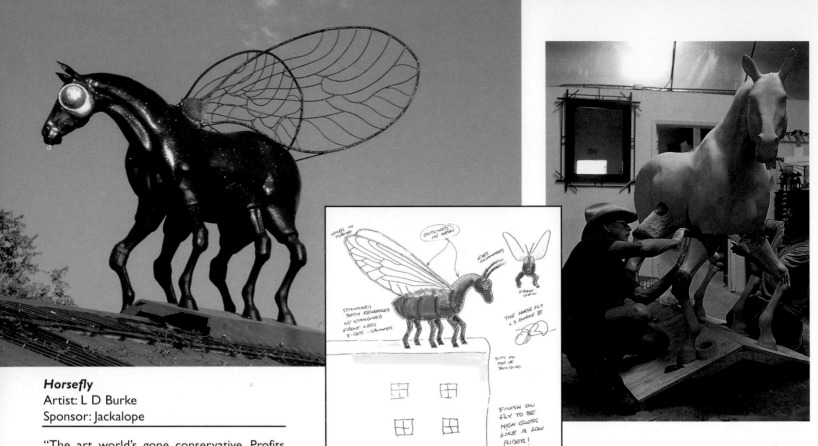

Horsefly
Artist: L D Burke
Sponsor: Jackalope

"The art world's gone conservative. Profits are down and serious heaviness is up. What better time to create something fun, silly and frivolous?

"The idea for this pony was 'channeled' (as we say in Santa Fe) to me by a live horsefly that took a chunk out of my backside this spring on the beach at San Padre Island! Believe it or not, that was the least painful part of the project. Right after I'd set the six legs, I awoke at 2 in the morning with the realization that the piece wasn't going to fit through the door to my studio. Several friends laughingly helped me move it to a space with double doors, but only after I chopped off two of the new legs. And then the bondo didn't set...And then began the search for the perfect 'bug eyes'...And then I had to figure out how to attach the steel wings...And then there was the neon to deal with... It wasn't simple, but then what worth doing is?"

Lucky
Artist: Jim Wagner
Sponsor: Margot MacDougall

Painting this pony was a way of exorcising his demons, according to this well-known folk artist, who realized he was addicted to playing the slot machines at a local casino, even as he created this commentary on the negative impact gambling was having on lives around him, as well as his own. After decorating the hide with gaming symbols, mounting a slot machine on the saddle, and painting the base as a Joker card, he fled his beloved hometown of Taos, broke and ashamed.

Eduardo Fuss, photo

Southwest Carousel Horse
Artist: Diana Bryer
Sponsor: Friends of Mesa Public Library

"I wanted to paint a Southwest carousel horse, but wasn't quite sure where to begin. So I started out with symbols I liked, such as the yin-yang, sun, moon, and stars. Then I added the orange Trumpet vine from my backyard, and from there the horse just evolved. The process was all very magical...."

Eduardo Fuss, photo

Hoof and Dot
Artist: Henry Leo Schoebel
Sponsor: Chiaroscuro Gallery

It was natural for this artist to use a dot pattern, a motif that he has worked with for a number of years. The dots are most numerous and dense to the point of overlapping on the face of the horse. From the head, the dots disperse, spreading with increasing space between them until they overlay the entire painted surface. It is as if the painted horse is a metaphor for the universe, the dots, not unlike stars, expanding ad infinitum.

Don Bell, photo

73

Jazz on a Hot Tin Roof
Artist: Kim Wiggins
Sponsor: John and Nolana Bassett

This horse—"installation" is a better term—flowed out of a creative process that grew into maturity through the interaction of people around the artist. His desire was to create something unique... something representative of New Mexico, yet symbolic of the arts in America as a whole. He decided to feature a New Mexico night scene on one side and a sunrise metropolis of New York City on the other, because "it has always amazed me how these two art meccas differ from one another, yet balance the arts of our society to produce what has become uniquely American."

As he worked he began to meditate on ways to reach across the lines and pull together more than one form of the arts. Music is a passion of his, especially Jazz era music. As he listened to old Billie Holiday classics, he began to formulate thoughts on the horse playing Jazz music on the rooftop of a Jazz club from the '40s... possibly with an audience of small animals.

Kids at the Assurance Home (the benefit organization for the project) helped him build the base. Another friend designed sunglasses

Eduardo Fuss, photo

and a neon blue musical note. A set of old bar stools obtained at an antique shop became the perch of the Jazz Cats. The saxophone was donated. He fabricated the mane from roofing metal in a way that produced a lyrical effect, as if the sound waves were flowing through the horse. Tenor sax music to an old Duke Ellington Classic, *It Don't Mean a Thing if it Ain't Got That Swing*, is mounted on the music stand. A silhouette of Jessica Rabbit (from the movie Who Framed Roger Rabbit?) stands singing in the nightclub window. A stereo is mounted inside the pitch-roofed base with the ability to play Jazz classics while viewing this interactive, and truly American, form of art and music.

Eduardo Fuss, photo

The Quarter Horse
Artist: Bill Curry
Sponsor: Mesa Technical College Foundation

Initially drawn to the design possibilities offered by a play on words, this artist, who was born on a ranch and raised working cattle on the back of a trusty Quarter Horse, "wanted a more realistic appearance than what other artists were doing. So I rebuilt the eyes, redefined the nostrils, added a forelock. And when the piece was near completion, I constructed a beautiful halter out of copper and applied a real 2001 quarter on the nose band."

Eduardo Fuss, photo

Storyteller
Artist: Ellen Alexander
Sponsor: Santa Fe Seniors
Activity Fund Corporation

The artist's background as a children's book illustrator and a woodcarver came together in this quintessentially New Mexican horse that was taken an extra mile when a friend from the Santo Domingo Pueblo was impressed enough to record some of the old Indian stories so the horse could actually "talk" to children.

75

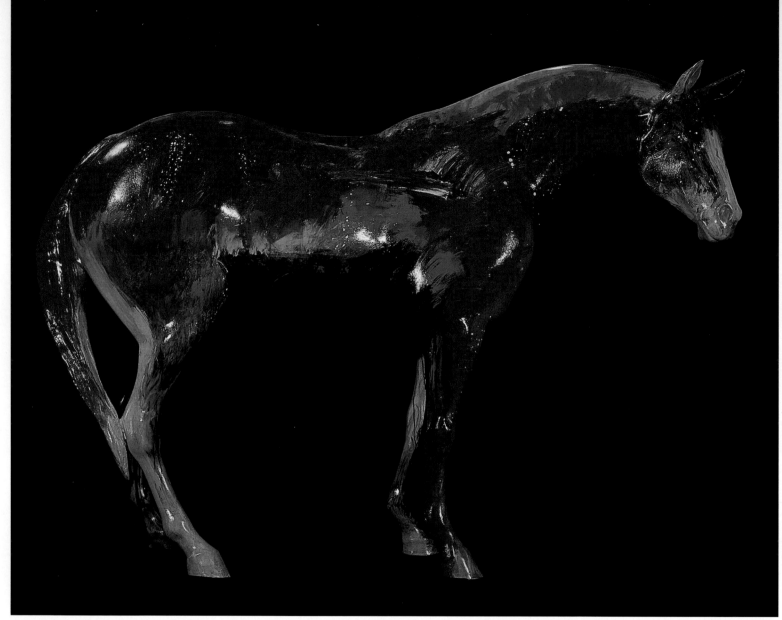

Eduardo Fuss, photo

An artist whose bold and unusual color choices epitomize the spirit of the Southwest, John Nieto was selected as one of the official artists of the 2002 Winter Olympic Games in Salt Lake City, Utah. He welcomed the opportunity to paint a pony as a vehicle not only for raising funds for New Mexico, but as a "reflection on the role of the horse since its introduction to America by Spanish Conquistadors. It made Native Americans a 'horse culture' with mobility. It provided transportation for all Americans before the automobile. And it played a big part in my own family history here in the Southwest. One of my great-grandfathers was a Pony Express rider. The other was a ranch-er whose cattle brand can be found on the left rump of my 'Painted Pony.'"

Trailblazer
Artist: John Nieto
Sponsor: Duane and Jody Shrontz

76

HORSES OF A DIFFERENT COLOR

Real horses come in many different colors. The most common colors are the Chestnut and Bay, which can vary from red to brown to black. Gold is the ideal color of a Palomino, though they too can range in hue from creamy yellow to yellow/brown. Paints and Pintos are flashily spotted. Appaloosas are leopard-colored, meaning spots occur all over, though some have dappled rumps. Lipizzans are white, Roans come in Blue and Red versions, a Dun is a red/tan color, a Grullo a mouse-gray color, and Buckskins are brown with a black dorsal stripe down the middle of the back.

The Painted Ponies cover the color spectrum, and are limited only by the palette of the artist's imagination.

Sequintial: A Sequine
Artist: Nancy Fleming
Sponsor: Minnie Wright

Seventy-seven thousand colored and iridescent sequins give this horse a subtle or striking aspect, depending on the angle of light. Seen either way, it is a striking "s-equine."

Lady Ledoux
Artist: Inger Jirby
Sponsor: Private Sponsor

An abstract expressionist painter with a gallery on historic Ledoux Street in Taos, this artist initially intended to paint a Rio Grande Gorge scene on her pony. But once the brushwork began, something else came out. A mix of symbols, numbers and letters that referred to other painters who have given Ledoux Street a reputation as an artist's row. Harold Blumenschein and RC Gorman, to name just two. Her horse also became more and more feminine, and with cadmium red stockings and gold hooves, earned the name "Lady Ledoux."

Don Bell, photo

Million Dollar Buckskin
Artist: Bill Crabb
Sponsor: American Pacific Mortgage

According to the artist, this horse is a "first in the history of mankind." It is covered with shredded currency—five thousand $20 bills, to be exact—that was printed at the Bureau of Engraving in Washington, D.C. but failed to meet government specifications and was therefore rejected and shredded.

Eduardo Fuss, photo

John Wyckoff, photo

Jackson's Jazz
Artist: Dianne Schlies
Sponsor: Peg Nelson

Based on the work of Jackson Pollock, this pony displays his controversial "abstract expressionism." It was created by the Albuquerque artist who painted Pollock reproductions for the movie "Pollock," and is based on Pollock paintings and Pollock techniques. Specifically, this design resembles the Pollock painting entitled "Number 3, 1949: Tiger." Jazz was the music style favored by Pollock, and selections from his personal jazz collection were featured during the retrospective of his work at the Museum of Modern Art in New York.

78

Thunderbird Suite
Artist: Joel Nakamura
Sponsors: Advanced Hearing Clinic,
R Bateman, P Epple, M Epple-Nibbelink,
MF McGinnis, G Sadler Family

"The Thunderbird glided across the sweeping plains of the West. A harbinger of rain and new life, the great bird was both feared and revered. The blink of its eye could cause bolts of lightning to flash; the flap of its wings could create thunder. It was said that a young warrior both brave and fast enough to ride his horse under the bird's great shadow would gain sacred spiritual powers. In the calm before the rains would fall, if you listened carefully, you could hear singing and the music of the Great Spirit....

"I chose the Thunderbird myth as a vehicle for this project because it evoked images of the horse and music. The legend of the great bird is almost archetypal throughout America."

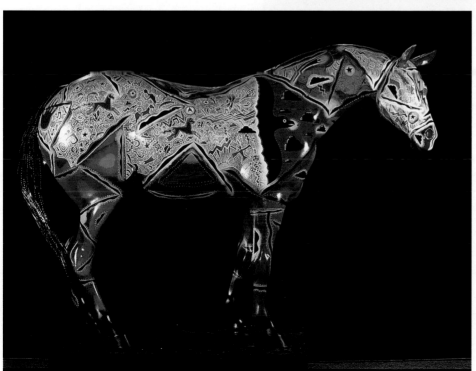

Eduardo Fuss, photos

Painted Pony in Garciavision
Artist: Rick Garcia
Sponsor: Zydeco: A Division of Yates Petroleum

Three-time artist for the Grammy Awards poster, this surrealist/colorist tries "to view the world through the knowledge that everything around us consists of molecules and atoms. Nature is not solid, and there are no straight lines. Though things may seem locked in place to our eyes, everything is in motion, changing, floating, growing, aging. Metamorphosis is the constant in my work as well, and I experiment as often as possible."

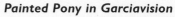

Shelley Heatley, photo

Eduardo Fuss, photo

Peace & Compassion . Ali MacGraw

Karuna
Artist: Ali MacGraw
Sponsor: Santa Fe Animal Shelter

A noted actress whose talent for creative expression extends beyond film, this artist saw the horse as "the perfect symbol of Man's connection to the Animal world. I chose to make a fantasy creature inspired by the fabulous horses of Central and Far-away Asia. I have called her 'Karuna", which is Sanskrit for Compassion. Compassion for all sentient beings, great and small, all over the world."

When this artist conceptualized a design that depicted the "unity" of cultures and nature that thrive in the Land of Enchantment, he had no idea of the saga he was about to embark on.

From the center of the horse's back the artist wanted rays from the sun to encircle animal drawings inspired by pre-Columbian drawings and carvings. On one side he chose to represent the predominant native tribes in New Mexico: the Navajo, Pueblo and Jicarilla Apache. On the other, he selected a tableaux that presented the Europeans who settled in this land: Spanish conquistadors, the missionaries,

Mexican farmers and Western ranchers. On the horse's forehead he placed a green hand, a gesture of friendship and symbol of the eventual union of cultures that took place.

To give this representation of "unity" the impact he felt it deserved, the artist decided not to paint his pony, but to onlay it with tiny Indian seed beads, applied one at a time. This stunning work is covered with over one million five hundred thousand beads - a feat that took the the artist 1,400 hours over 100 days to complete.

WILD HORSES

Serendipitously, The Trail of Painted Ponies 2001 coincides with another major event involving road travel and the adventure it represents: the 75th Anniversary of Route 66, the highway connecting Chicago with California, and crossing the Land of Enchantment. In fact, we have encouraged those who are celebrating the Diamond Jubilee by hitting the "Mother Road" to take a colorful detour and see the Painted Ponies.

In the same way cross-country travelers-by-car once motored across wide, open spaces, stopping at souvenir stands and tourist traps for American Indian memorabilia, we are inviting them to adopt a pioneering spirit and take a "trail drive." What awaits them is an experience that hearkens back, in an interesting way, to what automobile tourists encountered in the '40s and '50s, when roadside establishments offered glimpses of the indigenous culture.

Just as Native artisans back then, with an inventive sense of design, transformed common objects into popular mementos - often accompanied by wild stories to help make a sale - so have New Mexico artists in this project, through their talent, taken a popular form and turned it into something highly collectible.

Years from now, when families who drove The Trail of Painted Ponies revisit their vacation photographs, they will remember the herd of Wild Horses with affection and nostalgia.

Unity
Artist: Georges Monfils
Sponsor: The Sylvia Toth Foundation

Eduardo Fuss,

When East Meets West: A Printmaker's Pony
Artist: Susan Weese
Sponsor: Magpie Press DLD

Cutting up print images and putting them on another medium is rarely done in the print world. With this horse, a traditionally trained printmaker went to a new place, printing intensely personal images, inspired by New Mexico, on Japanese paper made out of the inside of long-fibered plants, and attaching them to the horse, all looked over by a Christian cross.

Eduardo Fuss, photo

Special Gift Horse
Artist: Kay Brubaker
Sponsor: C.A.R.C. Farm, Inc.

When the sponsor explained that he was very involved with the Special Olympics and wanted a horse with a Special Olympic theme, the artist came up with a drawing of a Trojan horse - Greece being the birthplace of the Olympics - delivering a Special Olympic runner. When the design was presented, the sponsor thought it was perfect because he thought every handicapped child was a "special gift."

Eduardo Fuss, photo

Eduardo Fuss, photo

Turbo Hay Burner 2001
Artist: Brett Chomer
Sponsor: Giant Industries

"The relationship between man and machines has long been a theme in my work. As an artist, I also enjoy the structure and repetition that go into the designing of powerful machinery. It was a struggle, at first, to adapt the kind of usual sculpture I do to the idea of a horse. But then I thought, 'Let's have some fun with this beast.' I started collecting car parts and playing with concepts and before I knew it, the creation of 'Turbo Hay Burner 2001' went into warp speed."

Five Card Stud
Artist: Gerri Mattson
Sponsors: Dorothy W. Queen and The Carlsbad Foundation

Before she began to paint her pony, the artist, a secondary art teacher for 25 years, drew up a list of words relating to horse. "Stud" caught her eye. She started sketching related ideas. This led to the game of poker. Gambling, horseracing, casinos, and lottery images followed....

Marv Shockley, photo

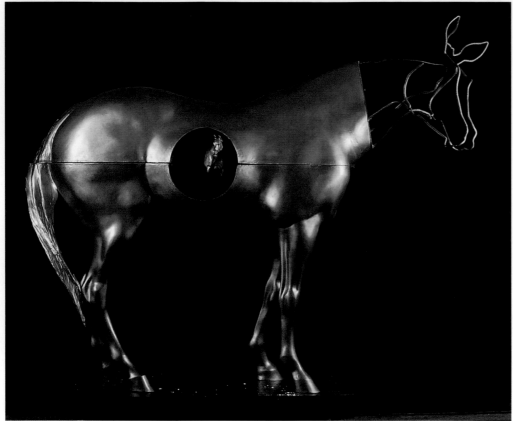

Eduardo Fuss, photo

Equestrian Self-Portrait
Artist: Karen Yank
Sponsor: The Munson Gallery

In collaborating with the already created sculpture of a horse, this contemporary sculptor, known for her bronze, copper and fabricated steel works of art, incorporated elements from two previous series: the Disc, and the Self-Portrait. The fact that she was pregnant with her first child while she worked on the piece shaped the concept.

Stare Mare
Artist: Nancy Reyner
Sponsor: The Cowgirl
Bar BQ and Western Grill

Questions about art, viewing and the way many of us are handicapped when it comes to our relationship to art, when we wish it to be only superficial, pleasant, and easily apprehensible, were spinning through this artist's mind when she conceived of her pony. The flesh-colored horse, covered with variegated human eyeballs, is mysterious and compelling. It is also perfectly placed in a restaurant courtyard where natives and visitors alike are busy seeing and being seen. Writes the artist, "The horse forces us to halt and ask, 'What does it mean to look?' It demonstrates that vision is more than just an image on a retina. We too see not just with our eyes, but with our whole bodies. As one viewer said to her entranced daughter, 'That horse has eyes for you.'"

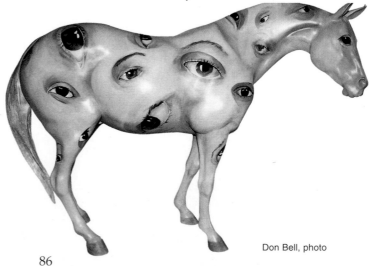

Don Bell, photo

86

Eduardo Fuss, photo

I Believe...
Artist: BC Nowlin
Sponsor: Merchants of Plaza Don Luis, Historic Old Town Plaza

Instead of painting Native Americans on horseback, for which he is widely known, this artist decided to create a conceptual work of art. While painting his pony in a public space, he would ask passers-by to write what they believed in on a blank canvas heart. The beliefs the public wrote down for him ranged from "I believe I will see my mother again," to "God, sex and rock and roll." He then decoupaged the hearts, as well as some of his own written beliefs, onto his horse.

King Tut's Royal Trotter (work in progress)
Artist: Steven Alverson
Sponsor: HorsePower New Mexico

A custom home-builder and furniture-maker, this artisan brought his fascination with Egyptian architecture to bear on the creation of his pony. "Many animals were worshipped by the Egyptians. The horse was not one of those. But throughout history horses have played significant roles in other cultures, so I wanted to honor the horse as the Egyptians might have honored him."

Pegasus (work in progress)
Artist: A-1 Master Mold & Casting
Sponsor: A-1 Master Mold & Casting

While producing the polyurethane castings for HorsePower New Mexico, the owners of A-1 decided to go a step further and have their team of talented artisans create Pegasus for the project. They wanted to show that not only do they reproduce art, but they can also create art. Every member of the staff had some part in the creation process - from fashioning the design, to fabrication, to the finished result.

Don Bell, photo

FREQUENTLY ASKED QUESTIONS

How were the artists who painted ponies selected?
Some artists, because of their celebrated stature, were invited to be part of the project. Many artists responded to a Call for Submissions published in magazines and newspapers around the Southwest. Others heard about the project and called HorsePower headquarters for more information. In a number of instances, sponsors or non-profits either contacted an artist first and determined their interest level, or had an artist in mind when they approached HorsePower. A number of art galleries saw the project as a vehicle for promoting their artists, and a few artists appealed to their collectors and rounded up the sponsorship fee that way. One artist even took out a bank loan to sponsor herself.

A preliminary design was requested of each artist—some submitted as many as six different designs—which was "approved" by HorsePower on the basis of quality and diversity. Designs that were too specifically commercial were not deemed acceptable. The ultimate decision regarding sponsorship rested with the sponsors, and the overall richness of the art in the project is a tribute to their sophistication and taste.

What is the size of the ponies? What are they made of? Are they weather resistant?
In an effort to distinguish The Trail of Painted Ponies from all other art projects that might feature the horse, rather than work with the standard equine forms on display at amusement parks and in front of western-wear stores, we commissioned a New Mexico sculptor to create an original design.

The horse is an American Quarter Horse standing in a relaxed pose, head turned slightly to the right. It is approximately 14 hands tall (about 5' from hoof to ear) and extends about 7 feet from nose to tail. It is cast out of polyurethane, similar to the material used to form boat hulls. The body is hollow, but the legs, ears and tail are solid. A steel rod inside each leg extends out from the bottom of the hoof approximately 4" to allow the horse to be bolted to a base.

Artists were given a recommended list of paints to use, and each horse is sealed with a UV-protective automotive clear coat to protect it against the elements.

Every reasonable step has been taken to assure the durability of the ponies under a variety of exhibition conditions. But it should be remembered that, first and foremost, they are works of art, and should be treated respectfully.

Will there be just one auction at the end of the project?
Currently, a series of both live and on-line Trails End Auctions are being planned. The first live auction of a dozen Painted Ponies is scheduled to take place at the Hyatt Regency Tamaya Resort and Spa, on the Santa Ana Pueblo, on October 20, 2001. It will be followed by a week-long Internet auction, which will lead up to the major live auction at the Lensic Theatre in Santa Fe on the evening of November 6. This will be followed by another Internet auction, with a final live auction taking place in early December. A public preview of the artworks that will be auctioned will precede each event. For details on the auctions, or information on specific artworks and artists, consult our website, www.gopaintedponies.com, or call HorsePower New Mexico at 505-955-9595.

How much will the Painted Ponies sell for?
It's hard to tell, but a number of factors will play into establishing their value:

1) The ponies are part of a limited edition of 120. Not 300 or 500, which were the number of artworks produced in some of the other cities where similar art projects took place.

2) There is a tradition of horses in art that this project is exploring in a unique way.

3) Each horse is an original work-of-art.

4) Each horse is one-of-a-kind.

5) The name and reputation of the artist will undoubtedly influence value in many cases, given that many of the top artists in the country are participating. That said, no artist in this project, no matter how celebrated, has painted a life-size pony before. This is a first for them, which makes the artwork special.

6) Some of the painted ponies have been so creatively and exquisitely rendered that the "name" of the artist is irrelevant. What stands out is the extraordinary talent and effort that is manifested in the art. The value of that can only be determined by how deeply it touches a potential purchaser.

7) And of course, given that the ponies will have been viewed by millions by the time the auctions take place in October and November, who wants which horse most comes into play.

How will the proceeds of the auction be distributed?

With the majority of the horses, eighty percent of the net auction proceeds is slated to go to the charitable or philanthropic organization designated by the sponsor, with twenty percent going to HorsePower New Mexico to cover promotional expenses and auction costs. In some cases, independent arrangements have been made between sponsor and beneficiary for the reimbursement of sponsorship fees.

If the sponsor is a business or individual, they have the right to claim a charitable contribution based on the appreciated value of the horse they sponsored. In the case of those non-profits who sponsored themselves, that deduction will be extended to the purchaser of the horse.

Who will benefit from the auction?

As any not-for-profit organization knows, fundraising is not horseplay, particularly when you are providing essential social services or important educational opportunities to your community. With over 400 not-for-profits in Santa Fe alone, the competition for the charitable dollar in New Mexico is huge.

In this regard, HorsePower New Mexico believes The Trail of Painted Ponies has something exciting and innovative to offer. By aligning businesses, the arts community, and not-for-profits in a partnership in which it is in everyone's interest to work together, we feel we are developing a new paradigm, one which provides businesses with a fresh way to market themselves. We offer the arts community a new way to gain visibility, and the not-for-profits gain an innovative way to not only tap into non-traditional sources of money outside the community, but bring meaningful value and reward to their regular donors.

The overall success of this project involves dynamic cooperation between all three parties. It begins with the selection of a good artist with a strong design by a business or individual. Of course, it is up to the artist to deliver a top-rate imaginative work of art. But the role of the beneficiaries is just as important. The degree to which they are pro-active, acknowledge their appreciation to the sponsor, promote "their" artist, and initiate marketing campaigns that enhance the perceived value of "their" horse, will influence the return on "their" pony at the Trails End Auctions. It is a project where everyone benefits.

Is this a one-year-only event?

No. In fact, a creative sequel featuring horses in more active positions and different sizes is in the works for 2002, and possibly beyond. Other variations are also under consideration, but for the near future, HorsePower intends to continue to produce artistically enhanced equine imagery.

A Call for Artist Entries for next year's event is already being issued. We encourage companies, organizations and individuals interested in sponsorship or participation in future events to contact HorsePower New Mexico.

Although this project will continue to spotlight the arts in New Mexico and profile New Mexico as a "horse state," an invitation to participate is being extended to artists throughout the Southwest and elsewhere. It is our belief that extending the "trail" to include quality artists from around the region will enhance both national and international interest in the entire project and continue to benefit everyone involved.

INDEX

Below is a list, by community, of the Artists, Sponsors, and Beneficiaries participating in The Trail of Painted Ponies.

ACKNOWLEDGEMENTS

The Trail of Painted Ponies has been made possible thanks to the generous support of our Official Sponsors, Artists, and Beneficiaries.

We would also like to specially thank the many people and companies in the state who have embraced this project by donating space, time and manpower. We will do our best to be specific, and apologize to those we unintentionally omit.

Governor Gary Johnson; Edson Way, Officer of Cultural Affairs; Janet Green, Secretary of the New Mexico Department of Tourism; LaNelda Rolley, Deputy Secretary of the New Mexico Department of Tourism; Terry Bumpass, Director of the Governor's Gallery, for providing the political endorsement without which a statewide effort could not succeed.

Mayor Larry Delgado of Santa Fe, for introducing a resolution to the City Council in support of HorsePower New Mexico, for following up with a declaration of May 20th, 2001 as Trail of Painted Ponies Day, and for his leadership in efforts to unite the community through programs that recognize the importance of the arts.

Mayor Jim Baca of Albuquerque, for having the foresight to embrace this project at an early date and encouraging his staff to find ways to make it a success in Albuquerque.

Frank Barber, El Centro Shops and Galleries, for generously providing HorsePower with reasonable office space in a premium downtown location.

Charles Padilla, for offering creative advice on the initial financial structuring of the company.

Del and Kathleen Mulder, Pak Mail, for providing HorsePower with its multiple mail services at cost.

Ken Bateman and Roberta Price, for their legal services.

Jay Czar, Director of Aviation, and Regina Chavez, Arts Program Manager at the Albuquerque Sunport, for their support of the arts and use of the Sunport as a venue for Painted Ponies.

Jon Nelson, for singlehandedly taking the initiative to involve Carlsbad in the project, and ultimately bringing two other Southeastern communities onto the Trail.

Mona Slayton, for taking the lead in Roswell and making it a prominent site for horses on the Trail.

Roger and Jill Goldhamer, for volunteering their support at Painted Pony functions from the very beginning.

Charmay Allred, for her multiple expressions of support.

Gordon Church, for his efforts to involve Albuquerque in the project.

(Clockwise from top) Horsepower Staff Don Bell, Mikki Anaya, Laura Solomon, and Meg Shepard.

The Carlsbad Foundation, under the leadership of Jim Harrison and Robert S. Light, who gave the project a financial boost in Carlsbad.

Russell and Claiborne Power, Frances Feezer, Dorothy Queen, and Mary Francis Merchant, for taking the personal initiatives to sponsor Ponies in Carlsbad, setting an example for others to follow.

Barbara Kelly, Publisher of Southwest Art magazine, for her interest in partnering with HorsePower to bring the project to her readers.

Bill Manns, Zon Publishing, for photographing the maquettes, and bringing his publishing expertise to the production of this book

Charles and Edwina Milner, for their faith in the project and singular efforts to promote it.

Don Barliant and Janet Bailey, for their advice, counsel and friendship.

Diane Loomis, for her belief in the project and assistance at the start.

Margot MacDougall, for her love of the arts and support of HorsePower.

Paul Goblet, Santa Fe Habitat for Humanity, for his recognition of the potential of this project to raise significant monies for a cause dear to his heart, and energetic efforts to blend the two.

Roger Copple, for his varied efforts to enlighten others to the possibilities represented by this project.

Wayne Mitchell, Signs Today, for his daily assistance at the Horse Corral.

Haines Gaffner, for his enthusiasm and help with the auctions.

A-1 Master Mold, for giving their best, and staying true to their word.

Steve Alverson, for taking an interest in the sealing of the Ponies beyond just a job.

Hakim, Muhammad, Ibrahim Chishti, for designing a terrific website.

Fabian West, for her wonderful graphic designs.

George Broome, for generously allowing us to use his space at the Guadalupe Center as a Horse Corral.

Paula MacDonald, Kiva Fine Art, for helping us in too many ways to list, and bringing four great artists into the project.

Susan McGarry, McGarry Media Group, for helping to shape the initial vision of the project.

Eduardo Fuss, for his amazing photography.

Last but hardly least, Don Bell, who like an angel seemingly dropped out of the skies, and has done everything from transport and install horses, photograph the artwork, clear political hurdles, and solve logistical problems. All with a smile.

Inn on the Patsey Marley

While Alta, in Utah's Little Cottonwood Canyon, is best known today as a ski area, being the second oldest in the American West, it is also true that it had a rather illustrious beginning as a silver mining town in the 1880s. Following the completion of the transcontinental railroad, a spur was soon built to the mouth enabling ore to be transported out to smelters in the East and Europe.

The trip up the Canyon was quite unique. Little cars, looking like a cross between a surrey and a toboggan, were put into service to transport both miners and tourists up to the mines. They were pulled up narrow-gauge tracks along the steep north embankment by horses and mules. Upon reaching the mines, the animals were let loose to eventually find their way back out to the mouth where they were corralled until needed for another trip up. Meanwhile, the cars carried passengers and ore down the canyon using only brakes to keep gravity in check.

Today, the Canyon is a designated watershed area for Salt Lake City and horses are no longer allowed - until, that is, Duane and Jody Shrontz decided to have their new ski lodge, *The Inn on the Patsey Marley*, sponsor of John Nieto's painted pony. The plan is to make the colorful animal the centerpiece of the bar (possibly to be called *The Painted Pony Saloon*).

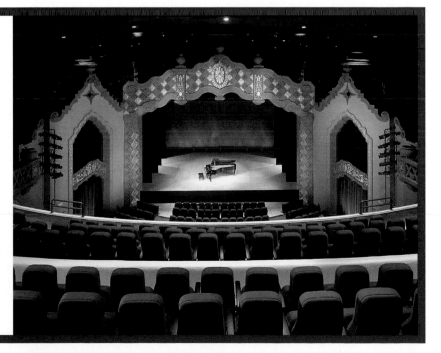

GIANT IS PROUD TO BE A SPONSOR OF THE TRAIL OF PAINTED PONIES. IT'S JUST ANOTHER WAY WE HELP FUEL THE FUTURE OF THE SOUTHWEST.

THE TRAIL OF PAINTED PONIES GENERAL STORE

Experience the Beauty and Wonder of
THE TRAIL OF PAINTED PONIES
New Mexico 2001

The Trail of Painted Ponies 2001 Postcard Book. A stunning collection of 30 full-color postcards that showcases the extraordinary and diverse talents of the artists who live in the Land of Enchantment. $9 + $2 shipping

The Official **Trail of Painted Ponies Poster**. Experience the beauty and wonder of 16 artfully photographed ponies on the official project poster, 18"x24". $15 + $3

Trail of Painted Pony Tile Collection. Two ceramic tiles handpainted by a Navaho artist exclusively for HorsePower New Mexico. Lovely enough to be hung on the wall, yet sturdy enough to be used as hot plates. $40 w/wood frame, $30 unframed+ $5 shipping per tile.

EXPERIENCE THE BEAUTY AND WONDER OF
THE TRAIL OF PAINTED PONIES
NEW MEXICO 2001
BOOK OF 30 FULL COLOR POST CARDS

TO ORDER: Call 505-955-9595
FAX 505-955-9600
OR GO TO: www.gopaintedponies.com